THE
CATHOLIC
HOME

THE CATHOLIC HOME

Celebrations and Traditions for
Holidays, Feast Days, and Every Day

Meredith Gould, Ph.D.

IMAGE

DOUBLEDAY

New York London Toronto Sydney Auckland

AN IMAGE BOOK
PUBLISHED BY DOUBLEDAY

Published in the United States by Doubleday, an imprint of
The Doubleday Broadway Publishing Group, a division of
Random House, Inc., New York.
www.doubleday.com

IMAGE, DOUBLEDAY, and the portrayal of a deer drinking from a
stream are registered trademarks of Random House, Inc.

Library of Congress Cataloging-in-Publication Data
Gould, Meredith, 1951–
The Catholic home : celebrations and traditions for holidays, feast
days, and every day / Meredith Gould.—1st ed.
        p.   cm.
Includes bibliographical references
1. Fasts and feasts—Catholic Church.   I. Title.
BV43.G68 2004
263'.088'282—dc22   2003060744

Excerpts from the English language translation of the *Catechism of
the Catholic Church* for use in the United States of America © 1994,
United States Catholic Conference, Inc.—Libreria Editrice Vaticana.
Used with permission. Excerpts from the English translation of the
Catechism of the Catholic Church: Modifications from "Editio Typica"
© 1997, United States Catholic Conference, Inc.—Libreria Editrice
Vaticana. Used with Permission.

Nihil Obstat: Most Reverend Monsignor Michael J. Alliegro, M.A.

Imprimatur: Most Reverend Monsignor William Benwell, J.C.L., Vicar
General and Moderator of the Curia, Diocese of Metuchen, New Jersey

ISBN-13: 978-0-385-51907-6
ISBN-10: 0-385-51907-9

146122990

For Polly Seitz,

blessed with the gift of hospitality.

She speaks with wisdom, and faithful
instruction is on her tongue.

—PROVERBS 31:26

$\mathscr{C}$ONTENTS

✐CKNOWLEDGMENTS

✐N THE PAST, it felt like quite enough to thank God and then to simply list by name everyone who provided inspiration and support while I wrote. Somehow, that approach seems insufficient for this book. Of course, I thank God. And I believe the Almighty knows better than I the true depth of my gratitude. It's the humans who probably don't know the impact they've had on my work and my life relative to this project. Mindful that words cannot fully express my appreciation, I want to thank the following people.

First, of course, is Elizabeth Walter. Her ability to discern the subtext of *Deliberate Acts of Kindness: Service as a Spiritual Practice* is what led to my writing *The Catholic Home.* She cut through all my flopping around about what to write next with one deceptively simple question: "How about something Catholic?" As I get to know Liz better, I imagine that she knew all along that this book would call me deeper into my Catholic faith.

And how blessed am I? When Liz moved on to Paulist Press, I was embraced by Michelle Rapkin, whose expansive vision brought this book to its next level of completeness. Imagine hearing your new editor say, "I think something's missing," when your manuscript is about to go into production. Well, that's what happened one Friday afternoon and blessings to Michelle for breathing through it with me. Michelle was determined to get me to think bigger. As I get to know her better, I imagine she knew that this book would call me deeper into my writing.

This publishing trinity is completed—indeed unified—by the ongoing presence of my agent, Katherine Boyle with Veritas Literary Agency. Since 1996, Katie has actively encouraged me to grow in faith and craft. May we forever continue to grow.

And then there's the rest of my life, all the people who play a daily role in my ongoing formation and, during the creation of this book, provided sustenance in myriad forms.

I have the great privilege of being a parishioner at The Catholic Community of Saint Charles Borromeo in Skillman, New Jersey, where faith and inquiry are nurtured in equal parts. I do not believe I could have written this book without the spiritual support of so many in my parish family and especially members of our choir whose intrapractice discourse (aka yakking) has enhanced my understanding of Catholic culture and devotion.

Our pastor, Reverend Gregory E. S. Malovetz, through the example of his own teaching and writing, has had a significant influence on my spiritual development, as has the wisdom and wit of Father James Tunstead Burtchaell. I am grateful for the spiritual support of Monsignor Martin O'Brien and the Reverend Martha Blacklock.

I give special thanks to Tim and Meg Keyes, extraordinary artists (and fellow cat loonies) who not only braved, but also understood my whimpering about creativity in service to Spirit; to Julie Clark for her bold ideas, steady encouragement, and abiding good humor; and to Polly Seitz for not only walking and talking this book with me throughout the summer of 2002, but for providing some truly memorable meals.

I want to make special mention of writer friends who may not realize what an important role they play in keeping me on task: Liza Dunkel, Regina LaPoint, and Judith Norkin. They "get" the process and they "get" me, which means I can call any of them about anything having to do with moving thought to type and be understood, even if I'm histrionically threatening to go bag groceries for a so-called living. Nancy Megha Buttenheim's exuberant support of creativity and Spirit has been a blessing for over a decade.

If you don't already know, I'm a convert to Catholicism. For years, I absolutely refused to use the word "convert," fearing that doing so would somehow fatally undermine my Jewish identity, despite the fact that it's an identity shared by Jesus of Nazareth, the Christ. So, imagine my surprise to find some of my greatest support coming from my mother, Gerry Gould. Her questions, concerns, quips, and steady love have allowed me to articulate what I believe, relative to who I truly am.

Finally, whenever it looked like there'd be a nasty collision at the intersection of identity and belief, I was safely guided through it by Bruce Reim, whose unique intelligence as a therapist and sensitivity to matters of Spirit as an observant Jew, has made it possible for me to become more holy whole while writing *The Catholic Home.*

$\mathscr{P}$REFACE TO THE PAPERBACK EDITION OF *THE CATHOLIC HOME: CELEBRATIONS AND TRADITIONS*

$\mathscr{T}$RITE BUT TRUE: Much has happened in the larger world of Roman Catholicism since this book was written and first published.

Pope John Paul II, the pope who was for most readers the only pope they'd ever known, died on April 2, 2005. Cardinal Joseph Ratzinger was elected to the throne of St. Peter on April 19, 2005, and is now the Shepherd-in-Chief, Pope Benedict XVI.

Depending on what press you read and where in North America you reside, priestly vocations are either at an all-time low or on the verge of renewal. Church participation among the laity, especially in the domain of parish leadership, is becoming increasingly necessary. It's also becoming somewhat more welcomed by clergy, despite the tinderbox effect this activity is having on conversations about the ordination of women into the diaconate, if not the priesthood. (You're welcome to guess my position on this matter but I suspect you'll get it wrong.)

Yes, these are exciting times for social observers and

culture critics who are writing about religious and spiritual life within the American Catholic Church. Some days my brain bangs painfully against my skull as I attempt to sort through it all. I'm having a blast!

Much has happened in my personal world of faith as well. First, I never imagined that writing *The Catholic Home* would provide so many opportunities to talk about Jewish history. Nor had I realized how much my commitment to reviving traditions that support Catholic faith is a coherent extension of my Jewish upbringing.

My parish-based talks about celebrating holidays, feast days, and the rhythms of the liturgical calendar at home have become focused on a core issue for contemporary Catholics: How can we sustain our unique Catholic identity, an identity that is as cultural as it is religious?

For many of today's Catholics, the ethnic customs that celebrate the birth, life, death, and resurrection of the Christ have been lost, forgotten, or abandoned for the sake of assimilation. And while folk traditions are neither a substitute for faith nor compelling evidence for reverence, they do help to stimulate and sustain awareness. We have to start somewhere.

I believe that celebrating Catholic customs in the domestic church can serve to reenliven Catholic identity in ways that Mass attendance simply cannot, although I, for one, miss Mass when I miss Mass. I could write much more on this topic; count on the fact that I will.

For now, I want to thank you for picking up this revised edition of *The Catholic Home*. You'll find some new material and updated resources. An index has been added at the request of readers—and my mother. I am grateful for everyone who contacted me with corrections. Your level of detail revealed how carefully my book was being read. I am especially grateful to the woman who took the time to write, "I don't care if you got a few liturgical colors wrong, I love your book!" I thank almighty God that no one wrote to complain about a typographical error so horrifyingly hilarious that I actually toyed with the thought of leaving it uncorrected. It has been corrected.

Even revised editions require support, and I've been blessed to receive it from Trace Murphy and Darya Porat at Doubleday Religion. I must also thank one of the many bosses of me, Ruth Harrigan, for enhancing my awareness of God's constant presence. I am indebted to Paul Schindel for his generous friendship and spacious love.

—Third week of Advent, 2005

$\mathcal{P}$REFACE

$\mathcal{M}$Y CHILDHOOD WAS rich with tradition, and I have the pictures to prove it. My father spent much of his life—and ours—taking photographs, so it's all there.

There's an especially wonderful image of me and Georgia Bresnahan, age four. We're decked out in little Easter outfits, including Easter bonnets and white wristlet gloves. Our black patent-leather Mary Janes point demurely to overflowing Easter baskets at our feet. I could show you portraits of my little brother and me, artfully posed in red flannel pajamas with a big red Christmas candle. There's at least one photo of my mother, stepping gingerly down the mini-staircase of our split-level, balancing a staggering tower of Christmas gifts. I could show you pictures of festive meals, although none depict the Friday fish dinners we consumed long after Vatican II adjourned in 1965 and many Catholics switched to burgers.

But if I'd let you flip through these albums on your own, you'd most assuredly flip out. Yes, I'm sure you'd want me by your side to do some explaining.

There I am from ages five through eight, regally costumed as Queen Esther for Purim. There's my little brother, his face beaming in the glow of Ḥanukkah candles. You don't have to look too closely at shots of holiday tables to see a braided loaf of *challah*. And the guy in black getting ready to bless the wine? You'll note how he's not wearing a Roman collar. That's because he's my cousin Jack and we're at my grandmother's house for Passover.

We moved out of a Catholic neighborhood in 1960, and from then on I was raised Jewish. This made a certain amount of sense since my mother is Jewish, and, according to Jewish law, that's what counts. My father, of blessed memory, was also Jewish, albeit a Jewish atheist-turned-agnostic-at-the-point-of-death. How I became Christian, let alone Catholic, is another story for another time. But that's what and who I am—a Jew in identity, a Christian in faith, and a Catholic in practice. I mention this because I believe it helps explain why I've written about creating a Catholic home.

Setting aside way too much fish, convent threats, and the fact my mother still mourns the death of "her" pope, John the XXIII'd, the major Jewish festivals created a structure of meaning for my years at home.

Granted, most of our home-based rituals and traditions involved food. But we also recited prayers. So what if they were from transliterations because no one could read Hebrew? After 1965, my mother thought we should attend synagogue on Friday nights, so we did so, under duress. Still, it was clear to me that schlepping off to services did not define Jewish identity. I knew I was Jewish—knew *we* were Jewish—because we prayed as we lit candles on Friday nights, during Ḥanukkah, and for Passover. Fresh flower arrangements showed up for the autumn High Holy Days. Passover preparations were as significant as the seder itself. Indeed, home preparations for holidays and High Holy Days always seemed more significant than any pew time we logged in synagogue.

When my grandfather died, all the action took place at home. Temple, schmemple. The rabbi came to us. We sat *shivah* at my grandmother's and Uncle Solomon recited the *kaddish*. Despite my inexplicable ability to recall entire portions of the Latin Mass, I knew we were Jews. Cultural identity was synonymous with religious identity; both permeated our home.

It used to be this way for Catholics, too; at least that's how I remember it. So imagine my surprise to discover, upon embracing this faith practice, how Catholics only a few years younger than I have almost no memory of growing up Catholic. If prodded, they're likely to spew forth a litany of complaints they learned from older siblings, my contemporaries, who fled the Church for abuses both real and imagined. Many of the complaints are about statues (idolatry!), the Rosary and novenas (vain repetition!), the crucifix (He's risen!), Mary (she's not Jesus!), the pope (fallible! a living relic!), and Catholic education (separatist! cultish!).

Much younger Catholics, starting families of their own, are fairly clue-free about how to create—let alone sustain— their Catholicism outside church, even if they attend weekly Mass fairly regularly. There doesn't seem to be a whole lot of "formation" happening after everyone is invited to go in peace. Sure, some kids are shuttled to Confraternity of Christian Doctrine (CCD) later that evening, but for the most part, being Catholic is confined to that place called "the church." When I was a kid, you knew you were in a Catholic home the moment you crossed the threshold, *any* day of the week. A powerful combination of décor and family ritual made that identity obvious, vibrant, and real.

I used to be the recipient of shrugs and darting eyes whenever I'd ask (nicely) how fellow parishioners reinforce their Catholic identity and practice at home. These days, this question is more often greeted with wistful sighs. I've noticed how excuses about suburban time compression have given way to the regretful admission that no one quite knows—or remembers—which traditions to restore.

Please note that no one seems to want the return of empty ritual. Thanks to my mother's pope, the Catholic Church underwent a radical self-inquiry during the mid-1960s that in many ways revived the long-lost, robust participation of the Faithful. Does anyone really want to go back to fiddling with rosary beads and staring at the back of the priest's vestments while he inaudibly mutters in Latin? I think not. But there does seem to be a felt longing for ways to reflect the awe, delight, and gratitude of living in and for Christ at home among today's young Catholics.

For centuries, the Catholic Church has offered members not only a rich liturgical tradition, but also an abundance of home-based activities to nurture faith and identity. Some critics have argued that external observances managed to eclipse interior formation; statues, scapulars, novenas, and the like substituted form for substance. Others have noted how, over the years, the trappings of Catholicism declined to the point of egregiously bad taste. Consider, however, that what cradle-Catholics find distasteful, annoying, or op-

pressive may simply not be that way for those of us who
come to Catholicism in adulthood.

I'm not interested in becoming an apologist for drek,
although I will confess a certain fondness for kitsch. I
wouldn't agree that some art "is so bad it's good." Yet I
would like to plead for a bit more humor in our lives. Some
stuff is just silly, so let's laugh our way to a deeper sense of
Spirit. I also cast my vote for mystery. Some stuff just isn't
knowable, so let's wonder our way into a deeper sense of
Spirit.

This book is for those who faintly remember what it felt
like to be Catholic, those who have forgotten, and those
who wish they knew. Here you'll find rituals and observances for holy days and feast days on the liturgical calendar that just may transform "doing" into "being." Although
I've omitted feasts that haven't been around long enough for
popular observance to emerge, there's plenty here for you to
discover and try. I'll leave to you to decide which are worth
reviving, which ones will help you appreciate the gospel
truth about God's infinite love and power.

$\mathcal{F}$OREWORD

$\mathcal{M}$EREDITH GOULD HAS written a profane book.

That may sound like a puzzling way for a bishop to begin what is actually a warm endorsement of Dr. Gould's work, but I'm using "profane" with its literal Latin meaning in mind, "outside the temple." *The Catholic Home: Celebrations and Traditions for Holidays, Feast Days, and Every Day* is a refreshing reminder that in the beginning the wall between the sacred and profane was quite porous. This was certainly true of early Christianity with its roots in Judaism. Before any churches were built and while Christians still "worshiped daily in the Temple," as the Acts of the Apostles reminds us, the early Church was being formed in the homes of believers as they gathered to share in the Eucharist. Our Catholic traditions always maintained that link with the "house churches" even when it was not consciously understood by those who were doing it.

The identifiable trappings of a Catholic home—crucifix, holy water, candles, statues, and icons—brought the sacred into the midst of the everyday, the profane. This comfortable coexistence between the sacred and profane, and the resulting sense of the mystical and mysterious, is an unfortunate casualty of our secular age. The liturgical movement, which had its origins in the early twentieth century, was a reaction to this secularism and was intended to revive that same sense of the "holy." The liturgical reforms introduced by the Second Vatican Council built on this foundation by reminding us that the task of worship is literally the "work" of all the faithful.

Dr. Gould has done a great service by providing a resource to that end. It is practical and helpful, witty and delightful, and spiritually insightful. Yes, she has written a book that is profane and also profound in its own way as it touches on those inexplicable, ineffable things that make a Catholic home.

✛ THE MOST REVEREND PAUL G. BOOTKOSKI,
BISHOP OF THE DIOCESE OF METUCHEN

For where two or more are gathered in my name,
I will be there with them.

—Matthew 18:20

The worship "in Spirit and in truth" of the New
Covenant is not tied exclusively to any one place.

—Catechism of the Catholic Church 1179

CHAPTER ONE

$\mathscr{T}$HE $\mathscr{V}$ALUE OF $\mathscr{T}$RADITION

$\mathscr{I}$N ADDITION TO being shaped by its historical and cultural context, every religion has a set of informal practices that have emerged. These customs support liturgy, sometimes softening it to become more spiritually accessible. They provide yet another vehicle for expressing faith. Call your religion a "faith tradition" instead and notice how rituals become infused with meaning that, in turn, reinforces your identity as a Catholic follower of Jesus the Christ.

Since its beginning, the Church has recognized, sometimes with great dismay, the customs of people it has embraced and, put more bluntly, conquered. Around the thirteenth century, the Catholic Church took more formal notice of sacramentals—signs, symbols, and activities that serve to enhance faith and identity. These include actions (e.g., making the sign of the Cross, praying the Rosary, novenas, nonliturgical blessings) and objects (e.g., Advent wreaths, holy water, medals, rosary beads).

Unlike the sacraments instituted by Christ, the Church determines the use of sacramentals, promoting some and demoting others at different points in history. Perhaps you're old enough to remember when St. Christopher was unceremoniously removed from car dashboards. A goofy example? Not to anyone who experienced and mourned his demise as patron saint of travelers! This example illustrates the Church's major concern about sacramentals and, by extension, folk customs: how to prevent mystery from slipping into magic. At what point does superstition eclipse substance? Since this is a book about celebrating ages-old customs, you'll want to give this issue serious consideration. To evaluate the value of any particular custom, ask yourself:

- Does this custom bring me into a deeper personal relationship with God the Creator, Christ the Redeemer, and Holy Spirit, the Divine Counselor?
- Does this observance reflect, strengthen, and sustain my Christian values and beliefs?
- Does this practice help me express my Christian faith and enhance my participation in the Body of Christ?

And keep this in mind: Don't reject a custom because it seems too enjoyable to be pious! Fun is absolutely compatible with faith. If you need biblical proof, search Scripture for references to celebration, feasting, and joy. (Hint: Where did Jesus perform his first public miracle? See John 2:1–11.)

YOUR CATHOLIC HOME

Were you raised Catholic? If so, what do you remember about your childhood home? How about your grandparents' home?

If you came of age before 1965, you can probably rattle off a list of items that distinguished your home as being a Catholic one. There was probably a crucifix over every bed wrapped, depending on the time of year, in either fresh or dusty palm fronds. Rosary beads hung from a bedpost or were coiled on a bedside table. The family Bible was displayed and, depending on your family's devotional fervor, opened to the day's Gospel reading. The Blessed Virgin Mother appeared on the family altar (if you had one) as well as the front lawn. Maybe you had a statue of the Infant of Prague (with outfits!) as well as one of Mary in your kitchen. Your whole family prayed the Rosary. Everyone said grace before meals *and* made the sign of the Cross—in front of company, no less. And that's just what you remember off the top of your head.

Chances are that if you were born after 1965 you'd be hard-pressed to identify many distinctively Catholic objects or activities in either your childhood home or the one you're creating today. The preceding inventory, parts of which probably read like a movie prop list, may trigger feelings of curiosity, nostalgia, or loss. What will it take to make your home the "domestic Church" it was historically intended to be? Take a tour of your home, asking:

- Does my home reflect my Catholic Christian faith?
- Have I created a place in my home and time in my life to celebrate my faith?

- What would I have to add—or remove—so my home strengthens the presence of Christ in my life?

It doesn't matter whether you have four kids or seven cats, Grandma in the upstairs apartment, or single friends within walking distance. You are heir to a venerable structure for creating a Catholic home—the Catholic calendar. Commit to marking time in alignment with the life of Jesus the Christ, and watch your own life be transformed.

Faith is a treasure of life, which is enriched by being shared.

CCC 949*

Getting Started

If you're reading this book, it's because you—or a well-meaning someone—has decided it's time to give fuller expression to your Catholic identity. Before you do anything else, you'll want to get or create a master calendar. You can either run off a calendar that you find on one of the many Catholic websites noted in Appendix E or visit a bookstore that carries Catholicalia. Somewhere, usually near the laminated prayer cards, you'll find a liturgical calendar that's snazzier than whatever your parish makes available.

Preprinted secular calendars generally note dates for big events during the year, but liturgical calendars also include

---

*Catechism of the Catholic Church.

saints' days and are color-coded for the season and feast days. Look for one big enough to include your personal notations about secular birthdays, name days, sacrament anniversaries, daily devotions, and other reminders. While you're at it, treat yourself to colored pens so you can make calendar notes in their proper liturgical colors! You'll need red, green, and violet.

As you'll soon discover, the Roman (or Latin) Rite calendar is a powerful tool for studying—and living—Christianity. Without a doubt, Catholics celebrate a greater number of events in Jesus' life than do Protestant Christians. Along with the Eastern Church, we have special regard for Mary, the Mother of God, and canonized saints. As a result, we are—or can be—very busy celebrating, memorializing, venerating, and adoring throughout the year. Following the Catholic calendar closely can teach you more—and more personally—about our faith tradition than attending CCD. And it can enrich your whole family's sense of faith, family, and tradition.

Technically, our liturgical year officially begins at Advent. It starts with this season for one obvious reason: Jesus is born; the Word is made flesh to live among us. And yet, as your own devotions deepen, you may find yourself "beginning" the year at different times, sometimes beginning again and again during the very same year. One year, it'll make perfect sense to start with Advent. Perhaps after experiencing a loved one's death, you may wonder why the liturgical year doesn't commence with Easter Sunday. If you earnestly celebrate *your* saint's feast day, you may secretly believe that the year should begin then!

In any case, this temporal cycle follows an unbroken

succession of seasons commemorating events and mysteries of faith organized around the birth, life, death, and resurrection of Jesus the Christ. Sunday, the new Sabbath affirmed by the risen Lord, is the key marker for determining:

ADVENT: Four weeks of preparation for the birth of Jesus the Christ.

CHRISTMAS: Season celebrating the birth of Jesus the Christ.

ORDINARY TIME: Weeks between the Baptism of the Lord and Lent providing time to contemplate and live the lessons of Christmas and to prepare for Lent.

LENT: Forty days of Easter preparation.

HOLY WEEK: Starting with Palm Sunday, a week of commemorating events leading up to and through the Crucifixion of Jesus the Christ.

EASTER: Fifty days of celebrating the Resurrection and Ascension of Christ.

PENTECOST: Celebrating the manifestation of the Holy Spirit and the birth of the Church.

ORDINARY TIME: Weeks between Pentecost and Advent providing time for living the lessons of the preceding great feasts.

Christian liturgy not only recalls the events that saved us but actualizes them, makes them present. The Paschal mystery of Christ is celebrated, not repeated. It is the celebrations that are repeated, and in each celebration, there is an outpouring of

*the Holy Spirit that makes the unique mystery
present.*

CCC 1104

At the same time, the Catholic calendar is organized according to a sanctoral cycle of days honoring men and
women who have lived extraordinary lives in the service of
Christ. By Vatican Council II (1962–1965), the calendar
was crammed with saints and devotional feasts, especially
ones to Mary. It was reconfigured in 1969 to reemphasize
the temporal cycle, relegating a fair number of saints' days
to local and regional celebration. Except for saints' days
providing seasonal markers (e.g., the Feast of St. Andrew
sometimes marks the end of Ordinary Time), we'll focus
on the temporal cycle in this book.* We'll also zoom in on
daily devotions that are not necessarily linked to the calendar, and also home-based ways to prepare for celebrating
the sacraments.

In sum, the Roman (Latin) Church's year of worship, beginning at Advent, is jam-packed with holy seasons and feast
days of various types, inspiring and requiring various levels
of observance. Some, like holy days of obligation, are feast
days devoted to Mass attendance, rest, and contemplative renewal. Others, like the seasons of Advent and Lent, are times
of fasting and penance. Virtually all have centuries-old

---

* Although several church-based celebrations (e.g., Baptism of the Lord on the
Sunday after Epiphany; Good Shepherd Sunday on the fourth Sunday of Easter;
the Sacred Heart of Jesus on Friday after the Second Sunday after Pentecost; and
the Transfiguration of the Lord on August 6) are omitted because they have yet to
give rise to home-based traditions.

Holy Days of Obligation

These six holy days of obligation provide opportunities to restore body, mind, and soul. Easter isn't on this list because Sunday is already a holy day of obligation.

Solemnity of Mary, Mother of God . . . . . January 1
Ascension . . . . forty days after Easter
Assumption of Mary . . . . August 15
All Saints' Day . . . . November 1
Mary's Immaculate Conception . . . . . . December 8
Christmas . . . . December 25

church rituals and folk customs that infuse each celebration—and our hearts—with special meaning.

THE VALUE OF RITUAL

Religious rituals—activities that help create a sense of the sacred—provide continuity and comfort for faith communities. God knows, there's no shortage of ritual for Catholics to learn and follow. The challenge is keeping ritual not only alive, but also vibrantly well.

Consider Mass liturgy, for example. Non-Catholics seem somewhat stunned by the unwavering predictability of the Mass and its constituent rituals. Predictability does not, however, mean forever unchanging. Before Vatican II, the Mass was criticized (by outsiders and insiders) for its seemingly obscure formalism and way of excluding laity. These days, Mass is served in local language, priests face the pew-bound faithful, and both men and women are encouraged to participate more. Not that any of this automatically guarantees *your* full participation. No doubt, you've caught yourself zoning out at least *once* during hours of church attendance.

At church, either the material or mystical can keep you from drifting too far. Perhaps there's something about the building itself—the vault of the ceiling or the unique olfactory blend of wood polish and incense—that invites you to become present. You might notice how a change in vestment colors shifts your sense of season. Sometimes the rhythm of the lector's voice recaptures your attention to God's word. At other times, music transports you deeper into the land of worship. You might find yourself mindlessly reciting the profession of faith when suddenly a word, phrase, or entire section comes to life—your present life—in a new way. The Host is held high and you are through Him, with Him, and in Him, in the unity of the Holy Spirit.

All of it—the physical structure of God's house and the rituals performed within it—serves to shepherd your meandering mind. But you face another challenge once you hear, "The Mass has ended. Go in peace to love and serve the Lord and each other." This is the challenge of bringing your Christian faith into daily life and, more specifically, creating a home that reflects your Catholic identity. Here's where traditions help construct and sustain meaning.

> *The spiritual tradition of the Church also emphasizes the* heart, *in the biblical sense of the depths of one's being, where the person decides for or against God.*
>
> CCC 368

CHAPTER TWO

ADVENT AND CHRISTMAS

WHAT DOES ADVENT mean to you? How about Christmas? What images, feelings, sounds, and scents come immediately to mind?

Let me extend my heartfelt condolences if you reflexively conjure up shopping malls, exhaustion, traffic noise, and only the faintest whiff of frankincense; not that I blame you for such Christmas crankiness.

There was a time, one that even I can remember, when Christmas was as much holy day as holiday. Outside lights didn't dot shrubbery until the third week of Advent and they certainly didn't change styles every year—they were always big, fat multicolored flame-shaped lightbulbs. No one bought a tree before Christmas Eve. If anyone did, that *live* tree was kept outside in a bucket of water until December 24. Home-made presents were as valued as anything shrink-wrapped. In this regard, the 1950s weren't as boring as we've made them out to be, at least not in the domain of holy day observances.

As I recall it, Christmas celebrations really started changing during the 1960s. By the mid-sixties, my family spent Christmas Eve at the movies and then went out for Chinese food with all the other Jews. This was probably as much protest against creeping commercialism as it was an assertion of our Judaism.

After I was baptized, Christmas became holy once again. Now I chafe against the time compression that would have our Christmas lights blinking by Halloween. My bah-humbug-ness has been offset by cultivating a greater understanding of this entire season, which extends from the first Sunday after November 30 through the Feast of Epiphany on January 6.

The days and nights before and after Christmas are rich with observances in seven-, nine-, and twelve-day increments. This is holy time within holy time that, fully celebrated, cannot help but lead to more profound delight in the birth of our Lord and Savior, Jesus the Christ.

It doesn't matter how physically, emotionally, or financially draining this season has become. You can, this very year, revive traditions that restore soul-nurturing images, feelings, sounds, and scents. The suggestions in this chapter show you how.

Advent

NOVEMBER 30 THROUGH DECEMBER 24
FIRST SUNDAY AFTER FEAST OF ST. ANDREW
THE ECCLESIASTICAL YEAR BEGINS (ROMAN CHURCH)

Established as Advent, a four-week period of partial fast-
    ing during the thirteenth century
Fasting removed by the Code of Canon Law in 1918
Liturgical colors: Violet

We already know Jesus will be born. Indeed, we probably know more about his birth than our own. Christ has come. By faith we're assured that Christ will come again. But that never diminishes the wonder of Advent, perhaps intensifying our sense of mystery.

During the four weeks of Advent (coming), we're expectant with awe; the season is pregnant with meaning. How can we not be excited? Still, after the baby arrives there will be no shortage of hubbub. Every few hours, the Incarnation will need feeding. Regal visitors will appear. The Holy Family will make the obligatory pilgrimage to the great Temple of Jerusalem (see Presentation of Our Lord, p. 47). And so, Advent is a time to luxuriate in peaceful waiting.

We reexperienced waiting at the tomb on Holy Saturday mere months ago, so it's not always easy to be right here, right now. The ancient Roman Church feasted. The Gallic crowd fasted. Our Advent observances embrace this sometimes contradictory jumble of devotions and practices. We turn inward. We mark time with calendars. We prepare hearts and mangers. We peer through the darkness. We haul out violet and pink candles. Our contemplation of everything leading up to this divine moment is enriched by knowing who—and what—is coming.

> When the Church celebrates the liturgy of Advent each year, she makes present this ancient expectancy of the Messiah, for by sharing the long preparation for the Savior's first coming, the faithful renew their ardent desire for his second coming.
>
> CCC 524

Bringing Light to Night

Nearly all Advent celebrations happen after dark. And since this is a winter holiday, "after dark" may be as early as four in the afternoon in some places. No surprise, then, that light features prominently. If you suffer from wintertime seasonal affective disorder (SAD), consider booking a vacation to someplace sunny during Advent. Noisy, light-filled festivities, starting nine days before Christmas, may be the perfect antidote to your SAD.

Latin American countries start celebrating the nine days known as *La Novena del Niño* (The Novena of the

Holy Child) on December 16 with evening Vespers and caroling before children take to the streets with firecrackers and other noisemakers. Similar evening antics are called "Golden Nights" in Central Europe.

"Rough Nights," beginning on December 21 (Feast of St. Thomas the Apostle) in other parts of Europe, include bell ringing, whip cracking, cymbal clanging, and parades featuring scary costumes along with fireworks to "drive demons away."

Another option involves staying home and going all out with candles on St. Lucy's Day, December 13. In Sweden, where winter is really, really dark and cold, girls dress up in white gowns with red sashes and, wearing crowns of seven or nine burning candles, serve saffron pastries, ginger buns, and coffee laced with aquavit liquor. Through the contemporary miracle of technology, you can find battery-operated St. Lucy crowns online, thereby reducing chances of inadvertently celebrating the Feast of St. Lawrence.

CELEBRATING AT HOME

Time to make a huge big deal out of your Advent wreath! Its form is set by centuries of European tradition: a wreath of fresh evergreens encircling four equidistant candles. Place it on a table or in front of the family shrine you created for All Souls' Day (see p. 125).

Three violet candles represent the penitential aspect of Advent. One rose-colored or pink candle symbolizes the anticipated joy of Christ's birth. Some people add a larger white center candle to represent Jesus. That one will remain unlit until the Christmas Eve Vigil on December 24, then lit again on Christmas Day.

One by one, each candle is lit on Sunday evenings during Advent until, by the fourth week, all four candles are burning. The rose-colored candle is lit on the third Sunday of Advent (Gaudete) to reflect the first words of the opening antiphon for that day's Mass: "Rejoice in the Lord always." (In Latin: *Gaudete in Domino semper.*)

Since there's no official rite, you're free to make one up! Or you can search for someone else's bright idea on any of the Catholic websites, where you'll also be able to find the daily readings (see Appendix E, pp. 227–233). Here are some suggestions to stimulate your ceremonial imagination:

- As you light each Advent candle, read the Gospel lesson for that day, or a Scripture passage recalling an event leading up to Jesus' birthday.
- Combine Advent candle lighting with opening windows on your Advent calendar, adding symbols to your Jesse Tree (see p. 18), and/or adding details to your crèche (Nativity scene).
- Combine Advent candle lighting with burning frankincense and myrrh incense to enhance your sense of the sacred.
- St. Augustine once said, "He who sings, prays twice." So sing as you light the candles. Can't—or won't—sing? Humming along to Advent carols and hymns will do

just fine. "O Come, O Come, Emmanuel" is especially appropriate (see p. 22).

· Combine any or all the above with praying the Joyful Mysteries on your rosary beads (see p. 213).

Speaking of singing, have you decided yet which sing-along of Handel's *Messiah* to attend? Just about every community offers at least one such event for amateur musicians during Advent. It doesn't really matter if you can't read music or sing tolerably well. These sing-alongs are packed with singers who can. Lip-sync if you must, but don't pass up the opportunity to be embraced by what is perhaps the most glorious musical tribute to Jesus the Christ ever written.

✝

In addition to an Advent wreath, you can also burn a Christmas countdown candle. This tall taper has twenty-five lines etched into its side. Starting December 1, the candle is burned down to the first line and to the next one every day thereafter. The candle is finished by Christmas Eve.

You can easily make your own by marking a taper or pillar candle. There's at least one entire aisle devoted to this activity at your local crafts store. Hey! Why not host a get-together on the Feast of St. Andrew to create these wonderful things? Surely, everyone who attended the rosary-beading party (see pp. 118–119) would love to attend, plus the folks who showed up to make pretzels for All Saints' Day, and also anyone who fancied those carrot bouquets during Michaelmas.

Even if you're an arts 'n' crafts whiz, you're better off

Praise God on the Symbols!

Every color, scent, and object is infused with symbolic meaning. The Advent wreath traditionally involves these:

```
Wreath  . . . . . . . . . . The eternal nature of God; the
                           king who is coming and will come
                                               again in glory
Ivy  . . . . . . . . . . . . . . . Clinging to God's strength
Holly  . . . . . . . . . . . . . . . . . The crown of thorns
Bay  . . . . . . . . . . . . . . Victory over sin and death
Cedar  . . . . . . . . . . . . . Eternal life through Christ
Violet . . . . . . . . . . . . . . . . . . . . . . . . . . Penance
Rose/pink  . . . . . . . . . . . . . . . . . . . . . . . . . . . Joy
Green (wreath)  . . . . . . . . . . . . . . . . Hope in God
First candle  . . . . . Isaiah and prophets who foretold
                                          the coming of Christ
Second candle . . . . . . . . . . . . . . . . . . . . The Bible
Third candle . . . . . . . . . Mary, the Mother of God
Fourth candle  . . John the Baptist, who called Jesus
                                      the "Light of the World"
Middle candle  . . . . . . . . . Jesus, Light of the World
```

buying an Advent calendar and saving your creative energy for Jesse Tree ornaments.

Usually constructed out of card stock, Advent calendars have twenty-three little windows and one big one to pop open day by day during Advent. And don't, for one minute, believe that Advent calendars are for children only. You go right ahead and peel off those cardboard panes. Underneath each are a picture and a scripture verse that tells the Christmas story. Start opening little windows on December 1. The big window is finally opened on Christmas Eve to reveal . . .

✝

So, what's this Jesse Tree? It's a centuries-old family devotion enjoying a comeback. Again, it's one of those traditions touted as having instructional value for children. But clearly, it also helps scripturally deficient adults locate Jesus the Christ within the lineage of King David, son of Jesse.

The custom is based on a passage in Isaiah. Take a few minutes right now and flip to Isaiah 11:1: "A shoot will come up from the stump of Jesse; from his roots a Branch will bear fruit." The Jesse Tree is hung with ornaments representing Old Testament people and events—Jesus' roots. The traditional symbols are based on the genealogy of Jesus in Chapter 1 of the Gospel according to Matthew.

You may use a real tree or branches without leaves and either order a Jesse Tree kit, or craft ornaments yourself from scratch. How many? One for each day of Advent! At the base of the tree, the first family—Adam and Eve. At the pinnacle, a crib for you-know-who. There's a scripture reading for every symbol (see box Praise God on [More] Symbols!). Start a tradition of studying these with family or friends, or contemplate them on your own. By December 25, you'll have a deeper, richer understanding of Jesus as fully human and completely divine.

Praise God on (More) Symbols!

The World Is Created (globe) .... Genesis 1:24–28
Adam and Eve (snake and apples) .. Genesis 3:1–24
Noah and the Flood (rainbow) .. Genesis 6:11–22;
                                  8:6–12; 9:11–17
Abraham (camel) .. Genesis 12:1–7; 13:2–18; 18:1
Sarah (baby) .... Genesis 18:1–15; 21:1–7
Isaac (ram) .... Genesis 22:1–14
Jacob (ladder) .... Genesis 27:41–28:22
Joseph (multicolored coat) ...... Genesis 37:1–36
Moses (burning bush) .... Exodus 3:1–10
Miriam (tambourine) .... Exodus 15:19–21
Samuel (lamp) .... 1 Samuel 3:1–21
Jesse (branch) .... Isaiah 11:1
David (harp) .... 1 Samuel 16:14–23
Solomon (crown) .... 1 Kings 3:3–28
Isaiah (throne) .... Isaiah 6:1–8
Jeremiah (tablets of law) ...... Jeremiah 31:31–34
Angels (angel) .... Hebrews 1:1–14
Malachi (trumpet) .... Malachi 3:1–4
Zechariah and Elizabeth (dove) .... Luke 1:39–45
Mary (angel) .... Luke 1:26–35
John the Baptist (river) .... Matthew 3:1–6
Joseph of Nazareth
    (hammer/saw) .... Matthew 1:18–25
Bethlehem (star) .... Matthew 2:1–12
Birth of Christ (crib) .... Luke 2:1–7

Sanity Clause

As long as you're toying around with tradition, why not give Santa a sacred makeover? Every year you have an opportunity to rehabilitate this popular symbol, possibly saving your own sanity in the process. Be the first on your block to restore St. Nicholas Eve (December 5) and St. Nicholas Day (December 6) to your seasonal calendar.

During the sixteenth century, the stately St. Nicholas, Bishop of Myra, patron saint of children in the Eastern Churches, was transformed into a boisterous, hefty old man with a long white beard. The red getup and beard happen to have been modeled (by Dutch Protestants) on the Norse god Thor who lived in "Northland" and traveled the skies in a goat-drawn chariot. How St. Nicholas morphed into Santa Claus is somewhat of an enigma, although Nicholas of Myra was known for comforting orphans with little gifts.

Amazingly, other countries manage to celebrate Christmas without their children pitching fits at shopping mall Santae. They do this by casting St. Nicholas as messenger rather than toy manufacturer, and emphasizing his status as a bishop.

European and Canadian Catholics follow the custom of having children write short letters to the Christ Child on December 5. These little notes which, admittedly may include requests for presents, are left on the windowsill for St. Nicholas to pick up and deliver. In South America, the little notes are written between December 16 and 24, then left with the Nativity scene's manger for angelic pickup and delivery.

In Eastern Europe and the Low Countries, St. Nicholas makes a personal appearance on December 6, dressed in a white robe, wearing a mitre and holding a staff. He expects children to recite the catechism or prayers, and is none too pleased with goof-offs. He distributes cookies, apples, nuts, chocolate, and holy pictures. Gifts are given during the Feast of the Epiphany (January 6). It's all very lovely and charming, and it does not involve superstores. An impossible dream, you say? Then, maybe *you* should try writing a prayerful little note to the Christ Child on December 5.

If making Advent wreaths, Christmas countdown candles, or Jesse Trees isn't ringing anyone's chimes, maybe baking cookies will. Home bakers, especially in Austria, Germany, Greece, Holland, and Sweden whip up batches of cookies during this time of year, especially for St. Nicholas Day and St. Lucy Day. For an international collection of seasonal cookie recipes by country of origin, check out www.christmas-cookies.com.

✛

The thirteenth-century saint, Francis of Assisi, usually gets credited for creating Nativity scenes. In the St. Francis version, everything is not only life-sized but also alive—Mary and Joseph, baby Jesus, and, of course, lots of farm animals. Real straw. Real trough. Real cold. Unless you have theatrically oriented friends and forgiving neighbors, these living tableaux are best enacted on church property. You, however, may have a more modest Nativity scene in the constitutionally protected sanctity of your own home. Not only that, but you can adopt the delightful European tradition of preparing the manger.

No, the "manger" is not the whole scene. The manger is the trough that functioned as a crib (crèche). Originating in France, this custom has children contributing wisps of straw to the manger each night. Each wisp represents that day's prayers or good deeds. The point, of course, is to create soft bedding for the coming Christ Child with these soulish gifts.

✝

Lo and behold, it's the evening of December 17. Time for the O Antiphons! You know the ninth-century hymn "O Come, O Come, Emmanuel"? It's based on the O Antiphons, which are brief, scripturally based prayers, based on the titles for Christ revealed in Isaiah. They're prayed before and after the Magnificat at Vespers, one each evening, from December 17 through December 23. And oh those clever Benedictine monks—the initials of the seven Latin titles for the Christ form an acrostic when read backwards: *ero cras* (tomorrow I will be there). Each evening after lighting the Advent candles, recite or sing these antiphons, then read the pertinent scripture passages. You'll want to add a recording of the O Antiphons in Gregorian chant to your collection of seasonal sacred music.

Making a Scene

Somehow your brother ended up inheriting the Nativity scene, the one carved out of olive wood from the Holy Land. Well, at least you got the Santa Claus collection, including the much coveted "bottle cap" Santa that's now worth a fortune. Still, you wish you had a Nativity scene, especially now that you're older, wiser, and into mystery. Finding one is not a problem, but try finding one you like! In the omega, you may have to craft one with shape-'n'-bake clay. Could be fun.

Also fun is the custom of slowly adding figurines throughout Advent. A watchful shepherd one day, an ox the next, and so forth. Mary and Joseph will, of course, have to show up at the same time, although you could spark a lively debate about that. Did Mary collapse by the manger with exhaustion while Joseph shmoozed with the innkeeper? Or was the enormously pregnant Mary there with him to beg for lodging? The crèche (crib) remains vacant until Christmas morning.

Please note: The Magi did not visit until after the Christ was born, so save those guys until the Feast of the Epiphany (see p. 43). Count on the cat making an appearance if your Nativity scene is on the fireplace mantel. If it's on the floor, the dog will flop down nearby. Let them! And offer up a prayer to St. Francis every time you retrieve missing Nativity personae from the water dish.

The O Antiphons

(with references)

December 17

> *O **S**apientia* (Wisdom)—Verse 2: O come, Thou Wisdom from on high . . .
>
>> (Isaiah 11:2–3, 28:29; 1 Corinthians 1:30)

December 18

> *O **A**donai* (Lord)—Verse 3: O come, O come, Thou Lord of might . . .
>
>> (Isaiah 11:4–5, 33:22; Micah 5:2)

December 19

> *O **R**adix Jesse* (Root of Jesse)—Verse 4: O come, Thou Rod of Jesse's stem . . .
>
>> (Isaiah 11:1, 10; Micah 5:1)

December 20

> *O **Clavis David*** (Key of David)—Verse 5: O come, Thou Key of David, come . . .
>
>> (Isaiah 9:6, 22:22)

December 21

> *O **O**riens* (Rising Sun)—Verse 6: O come, Thou Dayspring from on high . . .
>
>> (Isaiah 9:1; Malachi 4:2)

December 22

> *O **R**ex Gentium* (King of all nations)—Verse 7: O come, Desire of nations . . .
>
>> (Isaiah 2:4, 9:5, 28:16)

December 23

> *O **E**mmanuel* (God with us)—Verse 1: O come, O come, Emmanuel . . .
>
>> (Isaiah 7:14, 8:8)

THE IMMACULATE CONCEPTION

DECEMBER 8

HOLY DAY OF OBLIGATION

Established by the Eastern Church during the eighth century as the feast day "Conception of St. Anne."

Adopted as a feast day by Pope Sixtus IV in the fifteenth century.

Elevated to a holy day of obligation in 1854 by Pope Pius IX.

Liturgical color: White

Back on September 8, we celebrated the birth of the Blessed Virgin Mary. Now we celebrate the Immaculate Conception that would make her truly Mary, *Theotokos*, light bearer. This holy day celebrates the fact that Mary, by special dispensation, was free from the effects of Original Sin. The mind boggles. Logic simply won't work. I think we're best off relegating—or elevating—this Church dogma to the realm of mystery.

Celebrating at Home

What *does* make sense is the contemporary Spanish custom of treating the feast of the Immaculate Conception as Mother's Day. There, families join together to honor mothers and motherhood. Considering how mothers are pressed into mighty service at home and church during this season, you might want to treat yours to a special day of celebration on December 8. She could probably use a breakfast in bed and a day without laundry or cooking right about now. If you're the mom, take the day off before *and* after Mass.

Alternatively, since Mom is usually in charge of this activity, today might be a good one to shop for Christmas cards. You can communicate your faith and reverence for this very special birthday by buying (or making) cards that convey the sacred nature of this holy day. More specifically, this means skipping Santa, reindeer, and other images that have nothing to do with Christmas. And here's a bold move: Instead of sending an annual letter about how spectacular you, your family, and pets are, how about enclosing a prayer for peace and goodwill on Earth.

The "splendor of an entirely unique holiness" by which Mary is "enriched from the first instant of her conception" comes wholly from Christ: she is "redeemed, in a more exalted fashion, by reason of the merits of her Son."

CCC 492

CHRISTMAS VIGIL

DECEMBER 24

Inserted as the Vigil Mass for Christmas during the fifth
century.
Liturgical color: White

Mary and Joseph wander dusty, dingy Bethlehem, searching
for lodging. Her extraordinary faith and his extraordinary
obedience have brought them this far. Tonight, the impossible, the miraculous, the mysterious has become hugely
real. Where will they find shelter? During the Feast of the
Nativity, we're called to travel with them along this path of
faith and obedience (Matthew 1:18–25; Luke 2:1–20).

Our Christmas preparations continue right up to the
last possible minute as we make our homes—and hearts—
clean, warm, and welcoming. We herald the coming Light
of the World with light. Is there time to bake just one more
birthday cake? By midday, we may think there's much more
to do, but in fact there's just the waiting, a combination of
being and doing, which is certainly enough.

It's time, as midnight approaches, to sink into prayer,
gaze at stars, surrender to silence, and to listen for God's
first human cry. The Christ is about to be born and the
world will be changed forever.

The desire to embrace his Father's plan of redeeming love inspired Jesus' whole life, for his redemptive passion was the very reason for his Incarnation.

CCC 607

Celebrating at Home

So what if neighbors decorate their Christmas trees right after Thanksgiving. Try observing the tradition of waiting until Christmas Eve to put yours up. After four weeks of Advent wreath candles, Jesse Tree ornaments, and Nativity scene construction, trimming the tree on Christmas Eve becomes a special way to mark the passage of time.

And let not your heart be troubled. Follow this custom and your tree will be around in all its glory until the Vigil of the Epiphany—plenty of time for the cat to eat tinsel, the dog to knock it over, and for to you vacuum up prodigious amounts of dried-out pine needles.

✛

During the thirteenth century, St. Francis of Assisi insisted on all creation's right to celebrate Christ's birth. In fact, he wanted the emperor to order that grain and corn be strewn along public thoroughfares so birds would have more than enough to eat on Christmas Day.

You don't have to take to the streets, but before hunkering down to decorate your indoor tree, deck the ones outside with birdseed bells, chunks of suet, berries, popped corn, and nuts for feathered and furry visitors. Sneak a few treats to your neighbor's outdoor cats. Donate Christmas chow to your local animal shelter. Cave in to Fido's pathetic bleating for table scraps. (Just don't give these critters chocolate. What's treat for us is toxic for them.)

✝

Before starting on any of the tree business, commit to giving your house a thorough cleaning. Just because Jesus was born in a manger doesn't mean you may receive him in a sty. (Feel free to use this line with teenagers.)

Among Irish and Eastern European Catholics, deep cleaning is a Christmas Eve obligation. This involves household repairs (including repainting!), returning borrowed items, and finishing all work by sundown at the very latest. Given the amount of stuff we tend to accumulate, it might make sense to start tidying up as early as December 22.

Decking Your Halls

If you're going to go with authentically Christian symbols, you won't be decking your halls with much more than boughs of holly (Ilex). Its sharply pointed needlelike leaves have long been woven into wreaths to represent Jesus' crown of thorns. Its bright-red berries represent his blood. Indeed, green and red are traditional Christmas colors because they in turn represent eternal life and precious blood.

And don't forget the poinsettia, whose bright, starlike leaves have represented the Star of Bethlehem since the early nineteenth century. A native plant of Central America, the poinsettia was brought to the United States by the ambassador to Mexico, Dr. Joel Poinsett. Mexicans call this plant the "flower of Holy Night." (Note: Poinsettias are poisonous to cats and dogs.)

Finally, deck your holiday potatoes with rosemary, the herb long associated with Christmas. One old legend has it that Mary hung baby Jesus' swaddling cloths out to dry on the accommodating rosemary bush.

Line the path to your door with *farolitos* (little lanterns). In the southwestern United States, entire neighborhoods edge driveways, walks, and patios with *luminaria* on Christmas Eve and Christmas Day. They're traditionally crafted out of small brown paper bags, weighted down with sand or kitty litter, into which a votive candle is set.

If it's too windy out, or if you're generally freaked by the thought of burning candles in paper bags, you can make *luminaria* out of plastic cartons (gallon-sized) or tin or aluminum cans into which a design is punched (with a quarter-inch drill bit); even small glass jars will do. Or you can probably find electrically lit *luminaria*.

Some people display lit candles wreathed by holly at every window after the evening Angelus on Christmas Eve. This custom was started during the late nineteenth century by Irish immigrants to Boston. These lights are lovely, but they aren't *luminaria*. Add them to your holiday décor, but try *luminaria* as well. The magical glow of these lanterns will guarantee their annual appearance. Just make sure you extinguish all candles before leaving the house for midnight Mass.

✛

Invest in a gargantuan box of kitchen matches, because there are many more Christmas Eve candle-lighting customs to embrace:

- In Irish families, the "Great Christmas Candle" (*coinneal mór na Nollaig*), big enough to last the entire twelve days of Christmas, is red. Each family member gets a smaller white one; children receive small colored ones that are lit from the flame of the large candle during a little ceremony on Christmas Eve after the Angelus. The designated leader lights the big candle reciting the traditional blessing: "May peace and plenty be the first to lift the latch on your door and happiness be guided to your home by the candle of Christmas." Everyone exchanges blessings and good wishes. This might be a good time to exchange traditional gifts of fresh oranges, chocolates, dried fruit, or candied nuts.
- In France and England, a three-candle candelabra is lit on Christmas Eve to represent the Holy Trinity.
- Slavic families keep their large Christmas candle at the center of the table in front of the family altar. Ukrainians use a loaf of bread instead of a candlestick or plate to steady the candle.

✛

Here's what's universal about Christmas Eve dinner: It follows a period of fasting, it's generally lavish, and, if consumed *be-*

Making Christmas Customs Your Own

Finally, you've had enough of the annual holiday madness. You're on the brink of wearing a clutch pin announcing that "Jesus Is the Reason for the Season" on every article of clothing, including your bathrobe. This is the year you refuse to stand idly by as your uncle with the "slight drinking problem" staggers into the tree and insults your mother's cooking. No one's going to be ripping through piles of presents at your house. The TV is going to be o-f-f, off. This year, you're determined to "put Christ back in Christmas" while embracing lovely customs created by other people of faith. You may be able to pull off this noble plan if you're single and live alone. Otherwise, you'd be wise to adopt this twelve-step recovery slogan as your own: "Easy Does It." Here are some suggestions for introducing new, unfamiliar Christmas customs to your loved ones:

- Gradually add customs and rituals to what you usually do.
- Plan to retire a secular activity every time you add a new sacred one.
- Choose customs in alignment with your lifestyle. Some may look spectacular, but are too labor- or time-intensive to observe right now.
- Choose customs that speak to your heart. If you're moved to tears every time you light and bless candles, adopt candle-lighting customs. If you're moved to scream every time you roll out dough, let someone else bake dozens of traditional Christmas cookies.

- If you have young children, use customs as an opportunity to teach about the religious, spiritual, and cultural aspects of being Catholic. Study up so you can help them fully appreciate Jesus' Old Testament heritage.
- If you have sullen, reluctant teenagers, don't take anything personally and try to have a good time. If you have enthusiastic, adventuresome teenagers, thank Almighty God.

fore midnight (aka The Angels') Mass, does *not* include meat. Some families traditionally eat before midnight Mass; others immediately after. If you don't have an ethnic tradition of your own to follow, consider adopting any of these:

FRANCE: In southeastern France, a main meal of cauliflower and salt cod with snails, gray mullet with olives, or an artichoke omelette is traditionally served before midnight Mass. Elsewhere a huge meal, the *revillon* (beginning of a new watch), is served right after midnight Mass. The menu for this includes oysters and champagne to start; a main course of beef daube, blood sausage, goose, or roast turkey with chestnut dressing.

IRELAND: Supper, after a day of fasting, is a white fish such as cod, hake, or ling with white sauce and potatoes. The big pig-out meal, on Christmas Day, generally involves ham.

ITALY AND SICILY: The meal preceding midnight Mass

is a fish fête of at least three dishes, representing the Holy Trinity, and as many as thirteen dishes, representing attendance at the Last Supper. Most fish extravaganzas net out at seven, representing Creation, which is why you'll see references to the "Feast of the Seven Fishes." The type of fish and its preparation is regionally determined. Romans, for example, fry up a pan of eels. Yum! The meal generally includes shellfish, fried whitefish, *baccala* (salted dried cod), *calamari* (squid), octopus, *scungili* (conch), and stuffed baked flounder. Any or all the above may be simmered in a tomato or garlicky olive oil sauce, served hot or cold, with or without pasta. Roasted or pickled peppers, olives, spinach, potatoes, sun-dried tomatos, and *boccicio* (mozzarella balls) round out the menu.

POLAND: The *Wigilia* (watch) supper, served after the first star appears in the evening sky, is a meatless meal of *borscht* (beet soup) and an uneven number of dishes made with fish, cabbage, sauerkraut, potatoes, dumplings, and noodles. Poppy seeds are mashed into or sprinkled on everything. An extra place is set for an "unexpected" guest or for a family member who is unable to attend. The *Oplatek* (Christmas wafer) occupies a place of honor on the table. It's broken and distributed with kisses, prayers, requests for forgiveness, and good wishes before the rest of the meal is served. Pink and yellow *oplatki* are shared with pets, recognizing the animals' role in welcoming baby Jesus.

Plan to eat any or all the following traditional desserts, which are supposed to be baked, if not eaten, on Christmas Eve:

- ALSACE: *Bireweck*, a cake of nuts and candied fruit, served with gingerbread and compote.
- ENGLAND: Mincemeat pie, which really does include beef, beef suet, and chopped ox heart along with apples, raisins, candied citrus, sour cherries, spices, cider, and nut meats. And brandy!
- FRANCE: *Buche de Noël*, a cylindrical cake frosted with potentially lethal amounts of butter cream icing to look like a log, complete with leaves, moss, confectioner's sugar snow, and anything else you'd typically find on a felled winter log. You'll also need to nibble on raisins, marzipan, nougat, a variety of nuts, pears, dried figs, dates, crystallized citrus fruit, and fruit pastries. Tasting Thirteen Desserts is good luck. Good luck.
- GERMANY: *Christstollen*, a cake made with crystallized fruit and almonds.
- IRELAND: Plum puddings, fruitcake drenched in brandy or rum, mince pie.
- ITALY: *Nocciata* (triangles of honey and walnuts); *cassata* (a sugary cake filled with sweet ricotta); *panatone* (a fruity bread).
- SPAIN: *Dulces de almendra* (almond pastry).

✝

Make time to read the Gospel According to Luke (1:1–2:40) in the quiet, cozy comfort of your own home, perhaps using the text as an opportunity to practice *lectio divina* (the prayer practice of contemplative reading).

Irish Christmas Blessing

The light of the Christmas star to you
The warmth of home and hearth to you
The cheer and goodwill of friends to you
The hope of a childlike heart to you
The joy of a thousand angels to you
The love of the Son and
God's peace to you.

✝

Whoever is still ambulatory after lighting candles, eating prodigious amounts of fish, and reading from Luke gets to put baby Jesus in his Nativity scene crib. If you have kids, you have a couple of options. You can foster their sense of mystery by doing this while they sleep, so they wake up to baby Jesus. Or you can foster their sense of belonging to the Body of Christ by allowing them to tuck baby Jesus into his manger. (Don't forget the crib atop your Jesse Tree!)

Feast Day of Adam and Eve
DECEMBER 24

The Eastern Church honors Adam and Eve as saints; the Roman Church does not, but that hasn't stopped anyone from hanging on to the Paradise Tree.

After mystery plays fell from fashion during the fifteenth century, the Paradise Tree was replanted in the home. This tree was decorated with red apples to represent the forbidden fruit of Paradise and wafers to represent the Eucharist, the fruit of life. Today, in some Eastern European countries, apples are still part of the Christmas Vigil supper, but at some point in history, the wafers gave way to cookies. On this Feast Day of Adam and Eve, we remember how the Creator is reunited with the Created through the Redeemer, Christ Jesus.

CHRISTMAS DAY

(FEAST OF THE NATIVITY)
DECEMBER 25
HOLY DAY OF OBLIGATION
THE TWELVE DAYS OF CHRISTMAS BEGIN

Established during the second century as the date to celebrate Christ's birth.
Liturgical color: White

Traditionally, all holiday cooking and baking are supposed to be done. Now, and for the next twelve days, we're called to rest and relax. Mass is a must; then it's back to hearth and home to contemplate the immensity of what has happened and what is yet to come in the life of Christ—and ours.

CELEBRATING AT HOME

It's no coincidence that much of the traditional Christmas fare requires long, slow cooking times and relatively little supervision—turkey, ham, goose, duck, spiced beef, hunter's stew. Side dishes and accompaniments, like cranberry sauce and mint jelly, can be made ahead of serving time, as can dessert puddings. Notice what happens to the spiritual quality of your Christmas experience when *all* major food preparation is completed in advance. Mary had a baby; you shouldn't have to cook.

Spend the day listening to carols, hymns, and sacred holiday music. This year, pay close attention to the words. How, for example, does your understanding of "Joy to the World," "Hark! The Herald Angels Sing," or "Good Christians, All, Rejoice" change when you really zoom in on the lyrics? How about if you study *all* the verses?

The musical tradition of the universal Church is a treasure of inestimable value, greater even than that of any other art. The main reason for this pre-eminence is that, as a combination of sacred music and words, it forms a necessary or integral part of solemn liturgy.

CCC 1156

True Confessions: Christmas

Okay, so we swiped most of these Christmas customs and traditions from pagans and druids who celebrated the Saturnalia and Winter Solstice.

The holiday was originally "yule" (wheel) to note the year's turning. Yule logs and bonfires were burned to ward off demons. Before St. Boniface allegedly revealed to pagans the beautiful evergreen imprisoned in their Oak of Thor, there was no Christmas tree.

Mistletoe, which had great healing, protective, and conciliatory powers, was sacred to the druids of Britain. Ivy, before it was hooked up with holly (an authentic Christian symbol), represented the Roman wine god Bacchus and was a pagan symbol of partying.

Roman pagans used laurel wreaths to signify victory, joy, and partying. Christmas carols were originally pagan winter solstice party songs.

Baking trinkets, coins, or dried beans into an Epiphany cake was originally a Roman tradition for choosing the master of Saturnalia party ceremonies.

Exchanging gifts and greetings? Yep, you guessed it— based on pagan party practices.

CELEBRATING AT HOME

Okay, *now* start moving the Three Kings closer to the manger day by day, timing their arrival for January 6.

During the thirteenth century, church alms boxes were

emptied and distributed to the needy on December 26 (Boxing Day). Your contemporary twist on this custom could include using this time to:

- Make your annual charitable contributions. If you have children, involve them in choosing good causes to support.
- Engage in community or church-related service projects for the season.
- Decide where and when you'll volunteer your time throughout the coming year, then start lining up those commitments.

The Twelve Days of Christmas

DECEMBER 25 TO THE EVE OF JANUARY 5

You'd do well to heed all counsel to rest up on Christmas Day. The next eleven days are filled with feast days and holy days that underscore our love for the Incarnation.

On December 26, we'll celebrate the Feast Day of Stephen, the first Christian martyr to die for his love of Christ Jesus (Acts 6–7).

Within the Octave of Christmas on December 28, we recognize the martyrdom of the Holy Innocents, infants sentenced to death by King Herod who, after receiving news of Christ's birth, was determined to rid Bethlehem of all newborns.

If Christmas Day lands on a Sunday, then the Feast of the
Holy Family is held on December 30. Otherwise, this
feast celebrating the human family into which Jesus was
born, is celebrated on the first Sunday during Christmas. Consider switching your family's summer picnic
reunion to this feast day.

If Not Santa, Then Who?

Santa sentiments cover a wide range of feelings and opinions. At one end of the spectrum are those who see him as
a benign folkloric character. His eventual disclosure as a
myth and whatever childhood trauma results from that revelation are just part of growing up. At the other end of the
spectrum are those who see Santa as a vaguely satanic dis-
traction from the focus on Christ.

As you wonder how to tip the balance from silliness to sanctity, behold what parents in other countries have to deal with:

**Central Europe, France, Spain, Central and South
America:** The Christ Child (*Kristkind, el Niño Jesús*), ac-
companied by angels, trims the tree and leaves presents.
No one sees him do this. Gifts are opened on December
24, before midnight Mass.

Parts of Italy: The Lady Befana distributes presents to children on January 6.

Russia: Babushka distributes presents around the world on
Christmas Eve, like Befana. This is her penance for the

sin of providing lousy directions to the Magi on their way to Bethlehem, and for refusing to house the Holy Family during their flight to Egypt.

MARY, MOTHER OF GOD

(CHRIST'S CIRCUMCISION)
(NEW YEAR'S DAY)
JANUARY 1
HOLY DAY OF OBLIGATION

Established as Feast of Christ's Circumcision mid-sixth century.

Reestablished as Feast of Mary, Mother of God after Vatican II.

January 1 established as the New Year in 45 B.C.E. (Julian calendar) and then again during the sixteenth century (Gregorian calendar).

Liturgical color: White

God is determined to have the whole human experience and so, by Jewish law, the Christ is circumcised eight days after his birth. This is a liturgical sign of the Old Covenant God has made with his Chosen People through Abraham (Genesis 17:10–14). After Christ has died and risen, St. Paul will challenge the practice (Romans 2:25–28; Philippians 3) and Baptism will take its place as evidence of the New Covenant in Christ.

And Mary? Mary, Mother of God. Mary, Queen of Peace has birthed the Prince of Peace. Christ is our Savior, and today we remember that Jesus is her baby boy.

Mary is truly "Mother of God" since she is the mother of the eternal Son of God made man, who is God himself.

CCC 509

---

*E*PIPHANY

(ADORATION OF THE MAGI)
(THE MANIFESTATION OF GOD)
FIRST SUNDAY AFTER JANUARY 1
JANUARY 6 (TRADITIONAL)
HOLY DAY OF OBLIGATION

Christ's Nativity is celebrated by Eastern and Roman Churches. Eastern Church commemorates Christ's baptism by John the Baptist and first miracle at Cana.

Roman Church commemorates visit by the Three Kings and Christ's baptism by John the Baptist and the miracle at Cana.

Liturgical color: White

The tyrannical King Herod is disturbed when three Magi (wise men) from the East pop up in Jerusalem. "Where's the king of the Jews?" They've been following a heralding star and have arrived to worship him. This comes as news to Herod, who soon learns that the prophet Micah predicted Bethlehem for this event and sends the Magi off in that direction. They stop where the star stops. Ah! There's the infant Christ with his mother (Matthew 2:1–11). It's an "epiphany" in every sense of the word; check your dictionary.

On the Greek and Russian Orthodox calendar, this holy day of obligation commemorates two other events (Jesus' own baptism and the first miracle at Cana, where holy matrimony was established as a sacrament). We'll recognize his baptism this coming Sunday. Today's most loved tradition celebrates the Magi's visit and the end of this liturgical season.

> *The magi's coming to Jerusalem . . . shows that they seek in Israel, in the messianic light of the star of David, the one who will be king of the nations. Their coming means that pagans can discover Jesus and worship him as Son of God and Savior of the world only by turning toward the Jews and receiving from them the messianic promise as contained in the Old Testament.*
>
> CCC 528

CELEBRATING AT HOME

Inscribing the initials *C* (Caspar), *M* (Melchior), and *B* (Balthazar) above your front door with blessed chalk is a venerable custom in Eastern European countries. (Other cultures inscribe these initials on the back of the door.) The initials are enclosed by the year and connected by crosses. (e.g., 20+*C*+*M*+*B*+06). In addition to representing the names of the Magi, these letters also represent the Latin phrase *Christus mansionem benedicat* (Christ bless this house).

Polish folk tradition has it that along with palms from Palm Sunday and blessed candles from Candlemas Day, these blessed chalk initials provide a protection against disaster throughout the year.

✝

Incense is traditionally used for consecration. If you haven't done this yet, burn frankincense and myrrh, two of the precious gifts the Magi presented to baby Jesus.

Pebble-type incense burned on charcoal will provide the most authentic experience, but also the smokiest. (Definitely avoid this if you have asthma or other respiratory challenges.) Powdered, self-igniting incense is less intense and produces much less smoke. Stick incense is the least powerful, but can still provide a sense of the sacred.

✝

Okay, *now* take down the Christmas tree.

CHAPTER THREE

ORDINARY TIME: WINTER

SINCE ORDINARY TIME shows up twice in the liturgical calendar, I reserve my right to make this point twice: "Ordinary" is a reference to "ordinal" numbers, not time that's predictable or boring. Still, that doesn't stop folks from regarding it in those humdrum terms. I think this is especially true for the Ordinary Time between Epiphany and Lent, where in some climes, weather and light conspire to create drear.

Personally, I've come to love and appreciate Ordinary Time. So much happens during Advent and Christmas, on so many levels, that I find that my heart and soul need time to catch up with it all.

I understood this best one year when the liturgical calendar was so compressed (see Appendix A) that it seemed as if we had barely a week after Epiphany before beginning Lent. And it wasn't that I was miffed about cutting short winter's icy beauty. No, what got me nutty was that I just hadn't had time to behold the reality of Christ's birth before I was being called to contemplate his impending death. Never mind that we're called to be present to *all* of it *every* time we celebrate the sacrament of the Eucharist and especially on Sunday. Never mind that we're called to celebrate eternal life every time we behold the Crucifixion. I wasn't ready; it just seemed too soon for me to say hello, good-bye, and hello.

In those moments, the question "Where am I?" eclipses the more highfalutin question "Who am I?" Thankfully, the holy days and feast days of Ordinary Time in winter always pull me back into the cyclical nature of the ecclesiastical year, forcing my mind to surrender linearity so that my soul can experience embrace. I invite you to consider Ordinary Time in this way. Ordinary Time is observed from the day after the Feast of the Baptism of the Lord until the day before Ash Wednesday.

PRESENTATION OF OUR LORD

(FEAST OF THE PURIFICATION OF THE VIRGIN)
(CANDLEMAS)
FEBRUARY 2
FEAST DAY

First celebrated during the late fourth century as a feast of Our Lord in the Eastern Church.

Became a public feast of Mary for the Roman Church during the sixth century.

Called the "Purification of Mary" in the seventh century.

Liturgical color: White

Many events are commemorated on this, the fortieth day after Christmas. The Holy Family arrives at the great Temple of Jerusalem. Mary, ever obedient, submits to ritual cleansing with other new mothers. She has had a son, and this is the law. And because every firstborn male must be consecrated to the Lord, Joseph brings the humble offering of the poor, a pair of young pigeons. The lamb will be sacrificed later.

They are met at the Temple by Simeon, aged and devout, whom the Holy Spirit has filled until words tumble out of his mouth. Taking the baby into his arms, he is prepared at last to die in peace, because he has seen the "light for revelation to the Gentiles" (Luke 2:28). The elderly prophetess Anna welcomes the infant Christ. She, too, is suffused with the Holy Spirit. Her words of thanks and praise to God for this little one recall those of Isaiah the prophet (Luke 2:36–38).

Centuries later and for generations to come, candles will be blessed and lit in abundance on this day to celebrate the Light from Light.

During the greater part of his life Jesus shared the condition of the vast majority of human beings: a daily life spent without evident greatness, a life of manual labor. His religious life was that of a Jew obedient to the law of God, in a life of community.

CCC 531

CELEBRATING AT HOME

Traditionally, all the ceremonial candles for parish and family use for the coming year are blessed on this feast day. If your church no longer follows the custom, do try this at home. First, you'll need candles!

You could buy them, but why not try your hand at making at least a few (dozen)? Your local crafts store will have an entire section dedicated to candle making, and it's easy enough to find candle-making instructions and paraphernalia on the Internet. Looks like yet another great get-together idea for kids of all ages, doesn't it? Or just maybe, at this juncture, you're due for a quiet, contemplative candle-making session, one that will melt easily into a time of prayer.

✝

As for the candle blessing, here's one you can use:

> *Lord Jesus Christ,*
> *pour forth your blessing on these candles and*
> *sanctify them by the light of your grace.*
> *May our hearts be illuminated by your light,*
> *may our actions be guided by your light,*
> *so that when our lives here are finished,*
> *we may come into the eternal presence of your redeeming*
>   *light.*
> *We pray this in the name of the Father, and of the Son,*
>   *and of the Holy Spirit.*
> *Amen.*

✝

No joke, *all* Christmas ornaments, decorations, and anything else not taken down on January 6 must be packed away until next year. You can easily offset any reluctance to do this with the promise of a pancake breakfast. Pancakes and crêpes are traditionally eaten for Candlemas because of their sunny color and shape.

> If Candlemas be fair and bright,
> Winter has another flight.
> If Candlemas brings clouds and rain,
> Winter will not come again.
>
> ENGLISH PROVERB

For the Love of Christ

During February, just about everyone in the secular world gears up to celebrate love by sending cards, bestowing flowers, and eating prodigious amounts of chocolate in the name of St. Valentine. These customs should strike you as quite odd for a number of reasons:

First of all, the holiday started out as a pagan feast (Lupercalia) to celebrate the founding of Rome and the goddess Juno.

Next, you should know that there were at least two saints with the name Valentine. The one venerated on February 14 was a martyred Roman bishop. The other was a priest in Rome who sent notes of encouragement to persecuted faithful in the third century.

Still, you can count on harbingers of St. Valentine's Day showing up as early as Epiphany. There's no escaping this big, commercial "love" holiday, so why not make it at least a little more holy by contemplating what St. Valentine and other Christian martyrs have been willing to do for love— the love of Christ.

$\mathscr{T}$HE $\mathscr{A}$NNUNCIATION OF THE $\mathscr{L}$ORD

MARCH 25

SOLEMNITY

Liturgical color: White

Pssst . . . Mary.

"Greetings, you who are full of grace! The Lord is with you," declares the Archangel Gabriel (Luke 1:28). Are we surprised that the scripture story goes on to report that Mary felt "greatly troubled"? What could this greeting mean?

Well, it means that she—a virgin—has been chosen by God to be the Ark of God, the *Theotokos*, mother of the Son of the Most High.

Can you even begin to imagine being called by an angel? How about being called to so fully and completely serve God and humankind? Mary's answer is "I am the handmaiden of the Lord. Let what you have said be done to me." (Luke 1:38). Mary says "yes" and the Word becomes flesh.

> *The gospel accounts understand the virginal conception of Jesus as a divine work that surpasses all human understanding and possibility. . . . The meaning of this event is accessible only to faith, which understands in it the "connection of these mysteries within another" in the totality of Christ's mysteries, from his Incarnation to his Passover.*
>
> CCC 497, 498

CELEBRATING AT HOME

Even though Mary's "yes" was wholehearted and emphatic, it's customary for French and Scandinavian Catholics to celebrate the Annunciation of the Lord with *waffles* ("waffle," get it?) piled high with whipped cream! Yes, you may certainly add strawberries.

✝

Legend has it that the Archangel Gabriel appeared to Mary at 6 P.M. which is why the Angelus is recited to honor the

Incarnation at this hour. If there was ever a day to recite this beautiful prayer, this is it. And, you simply must surround the recitation of this prayer with the sound of beautiful, sparkling bright bells.

The Angelus

V. The angel of the Lord spoke to Mary.

R. And she conceived by the Holy Spirit. Hail Mary . . .

V. Behold the handmaiden of the Lord.

R. Let it be done to me according to your word. Hail Mary . . .

V. And the Word became flesh

R. And lived among us. Hail Mary . . .

V. Pray for us, O holy Mother of God,

R. That we may be made worthy of the promises of Christ.

V. Let us pray. Lord, fill our hearts with your grace: Once, through the message of an angel you revealed the Incarnation of your Son; now, through his suffering and death on the Cross lead us to the glory of his Resurrection. We ask this through Christ our Lord.

R. Amen.

CHAPTER FOUR

LENT AND EASTER

*I*T'S NOT TOO MUCH of a stretch to note how, like the seasons of Advent and Christmas, Lent and Easter have become secularized. I'll spare you my rant about how and why Easter, the holiest day on the liturgical calendar, has declined in reverence. And don't get me started about how I think Christians ought to be paying more attention to the Jewish feast of Passover.

I'm hardly one to talk. You'll recall from the Preface to this book that I, during my formative years, was stuffed into an adorable Easter outfit by my Jewish mother. I'll add here that I treasured the diorama eggs I received from Catholic neighbors. Yet, even as a child I was deep (translation: morbid) enough to wrench my attention away from the chocolate bunnies and zoom in on the season's gut-wrenching betrayal stories.

The other part—the part about resurrection of the dead and the life of the world to come—wouldn't emerge in my consciousness for decades. And I believe that what my emerging awareness of what Christ triumphant meant for *me* is what led to my baptism. By the way, my (full-immersion) baptism happened not during Easter (as is Catholic tradition) but at the end of December. In practical terms, this meant I'd had nearly four months of Jesus in my heart by the time my first Easter as a baptized Christian rolled around. I might have predicted changes in my understanding of Lent and Easter. I did not, however, fully anticipate how I'd feel about Passover—especially in relation to the Triduum.

Simply put, I'm a wreck during Holy Week, but that's another story. Here, I'll point out that if there's ever a time during the liturgical year to appreciate the profound impact of Christ on the world then and now, it's during Lent, Easter, and the Feast of Pentecost fifty days after Easter. You'll see what I mean if you adopt the traditions I've included in this chapter.

℘RE-ℒENT

FROM SEPTUAGESIMA SUNDAY TO ASH WEDNESDAY
AS EARLY AS MID-JANUARY, AS LATE AS FEBRUARY

Established as a separate season of preparation in or after the eighth century.
Liturgical color: Green

Even though Lent is itself a time of preparation, a number of customs help us preprepare. Pre-Lent preparation is most visibly and dramatically evident in what we do with food—cutting down intake and really having meatless meals on Fridays.

According to custom, the three weeks prior to Lent are ones of extreme celebration. The weeklong festivities before Ash Wednesday are called "carnival" time because, in Latin, *carne levarium* means "removal of meat." Beginning in the seventeenth century, purportedly mature Christians would go a little wild visiting friends, carrying on at masquerade balls, gambling, and having water fights. Bishops would occasionally try to prohibit this excessive fun, with little or no success.

These days, we ready up for Lent by bidding good-bye to the Alleluia until Easter Sunday and heading in the direction of fasting and abstinence. For three weeks, we get ready by weaning ourselves away from all that distracts us from Lenten self-examination, contemplation, repentance, contrition, and good works.

CELEBRATING AT HOME

Your Lenten examination of conscience will be more rigorous if you commit it to writing; even more so if you write by hand. Handwriting is a slower way to record thoughts and feelings, which is exactly the point. Also, the physical act of writing things out seems to help connect body, mind, and spirit.

Set some time aside during pre-Lenten frivolity to buy a special notebook, and then use it to record your responses to these heart-provoking questions:

- Am I loving, honest, tolerant, generous, patient, kind, trustworthy?
- In what ways do I represent the love of Christ? Do I live my faith?
- When, how, and why am I angry, mean-spirited, stingy, envious, hostile?
- What actions of mine have hurt others?
- For what do I want forgiveness?
- From whom do I need to ask forgiveness?
- How have I hurt others by not taking appropriate action?
- Whom do I need to forgive?
- What do I allow to separate me from the love of Christ?
- How can I open my heart, cleanse my soul, and deepen my faith?

Although we're called to serve others throughout the year, Lent is a special season of almsgiving. Most people think the term refers exclusively to giving money. It doesn't. Pre-Lent would be a good time to consider where you can perform deliberate acts of kindness, sharing your time and talents with those in need. Start by checking out your parish social outreach ministry. If nothing there appeals to you, pursue that volunteer work that's been on your "to do" list for ages. My book, *Deliberate Acts of Kindness: Service as a Spiritual Practice,* will give you more ideas.

SHROVE TUESDAY

Weeks of food antics peak on the last day of pre-Lent, Shrove Tuesday (aka Mardi Gras, Fat Tuesday, Fasten's Eve, or *Fastnacht*). The name "Shrove" derives from the customary pre-Lenten "shrift" (confession), but it's mostly known for gluttony.

By now, we're supposed to have had our last deluxe bacon cheeseburger for the duration. In the old days, eggs, butter, fat, milk, and cheese were also considered verboten during Lent, so Shrove Tuesday was devoted to emptying the larder. For old times' sake, you might consider following this tradition, which happens also to be a healthier way of eating.

Shrove Tuesday is not an official liturgical holiday, but a funky way to mark the moveable feast of Easter.

CELEBRATING AT HOME

Flipping out over pancakes is so universal on Shrove Tuesday that the holiday is sometimes called "Pancake Tuesday." This morning, instead of popping frozen anything into the toaster, make stacks of flapjacks the old-fashioned way. Griddlecakes are an easy, delicious way to use up eggs, milk, butter, and fat (like bacon drippings).

If making them first thing in the morning seems too daunting, serve them up for dinner. In England, Pancake Day is celebrated with races at which women over the age of sixteen, frying pans in hand, trot over 415 yards while tossing pancakes over at least three times. Zoom in on *that* before muttering naughty words as you scrub batter splatters off your stove.

✝

In New Orleans, one of the less over-the-top Mardi Gras customs involves baking King's Cake, a yeasty, buttery confection flavored with lemon zest, cinnamon, and nutmeg decorated with purple, yellow, and green icing—and these aren't even its most distinguishing characteristics!

A tiny doll of the baby Jesus is baked inside the cake, which, when done, is doled out in huge slices. Whoever gets the slice with the doll provides the King's Cake the following year. (Brush up on the Heimlich maneuver before serving this.) For an authentic King's Cake recipe check out the one at www.theholidayspot.com/mardigras.

✝

Hodgepodge, a stewlike conglomeration, is a traditional Shrove Tuesday dish among Eastern Europeans. It's generally created by mixing peas, beans, and potatoes with the last of the pig parts (e.g., feet, tail, head) thrown in for extra flavoring.

Simple vegetarian soups are also traditional throughout Lent, and each nationality has developed its own Lenten specialty. Consider slurping any—or all—of the following for the next forty days:

EASTERN EUROPE: Vegetable-based split pea soup.

FRANCE: Onion soup, of course! Call it *Zuppa Magna di Cipolle* and you can claim it's Italian.

GREECE: Tomato soup. (In barely any more time than it takes to open a can, you can easily create the real thing.)

ITALY: *Brodo Magro di Digiuno* is made with leeks, onions, carrots, cabbage, and lentils, flavored with sage and bay leaf. Strained, it's a rich broth for other soups or to use with rice or pasta. Puréed, it's a hearty soup.

RUSSIA: Borscht (beet soup) with mushrooms or barley. Sauerkraut and mushroom soup. Cabbage, potato, carrot, and barley soup.

Eastern Orthodox Church adherents still observe relatively strict fasting—relative to what most Roman Rite Catholics do—during Lent. Check out www.orthodoxchurch.com/fastdays.htm to see what rigorous fasting looks like. Go to Orthodox Christian Information Center at www.orthodoxinfo.com to find tasty Lenten soup and stew recipes for when you do eat. And, if you decide to go the complete vegetarian route for the next forty days, check out Mollie Katzen's *The Moosewood Cookbook* (Ten Speed Press, 1977). Published over two decades ago, it's still one of the best resources for vegetarian recipes and especially wonderful soups.

✝

Strange but true: The pretzel is the oldest, traditional, authentically Christian Lenten bread. Some food historians trace its origin back to Roman Christians of the fifth century. Others insist that monks in southern France, or maybe it was northern Italy, cooked up this egg- and butter-free snack in A.D. 610. The former called them *bracellae*, Latin for "little arms"; the latter called them *pretiola*, Latin for "little reward."

In either account, the dough configuration represents

arms folded in prayer and the three holes represent the Trinity. Thus, you may eat these with impunity, but not gluttony, throughout Lent. In fact, having pretzels around may be inspiring. (For recipe, see p. 123.)

So where does "pretzel" come from? Germans, who called these breads *bretzel* ("little bread"). And here's information you'll need for future quiz shows: Palatine Germans, who would become known as the Pennsylvania Dutch, imported pretzels to the United States in 1710.

Giving Up for Lent

"What are you giving up for Lent?" Who hasn't heard this seasonal greeting? If the response isn't chocolate, it's some other indulgence. Movies. Gummi Bears. Trashy novels. Clothes shopping. Occasionally, someone will dare forgo watching TV.

Conventional wisdom has it that deprivation in the name of sacrifice—swearing off life's pleasures for forty days—will somehow intimately connect us with the Crucifixion. Maybe. For kids, probably. Adults have more sophisticated and spiritually challenging options.

Is God calling us to sacrifice? Or are we being called to cultivate a supercharged awareness of the times and ways we separate ourselves from God because of the things we want—or the stuff we do?

When it comes to pleasing God, sacrifice may *not* be the way to go. Take a look at Micah 6:8. When it's his turn to be spoken through by the Holy Spirit, this Old Testament prophet says, Get it: No more burnt offerings. No more slaughtered calves. Don't bother pouring buckets of precious oils on the altar. I won't even ask you to expiate your sins by sacrificing *your* firstborn. Instead, we're called "to act justly, to love tenderly, and to walk humbly with your God."

What would you have to stop, surrender, or abandon to live like this during Lent? What would Lent be like if you gave up vengeance, gossip, sarcasm, or stinginess instead of chocolate? What would *you* be like?

Another pre-Lent tradition, having nothing ostensibly to do with food, involves a slight folk obsession with bees in Eastern Europe. On Shrove Tuesday, children, costumed as bees, buzz in tubs while being drenched with buckets of water. God only knows why, and the Archangel Gabriel has yet to deliver this information. Still, it might be sweet amusement to dress up like a bee, buzz, skip the water part, and eat honey-dipped fruit. Kids would love this, especially if combined with the traditional sledding party for this day.

> *It is important for every person to be sufficiently present to himself to hear and follow the voice of his conscience. This requirement of interiority is all the more necessary as life often distracts us from any reflection, self-examination or introspection.*
>
> CCC 1779

THE FORTY DAYS OF LENT

ASH WEDNESDAY THROUGH HOLY THURSDAY

The Roman Church skips Sundays when calculating the length of Lent. Lent is always the seventh Wednesday before Easter.

The Eastern Church includes Sundays when calculating the length of the Great Lent.

Liturgical color: Violet

ASH WEDNESDAY

Day of Ashes (*Dies Cinerum*) originated during the sixth century.

Extended to the entire Western Church in the eleventh century.

At the beginning of his ministry on earth, Jesus the Christ is led by the Spirit into the desert where he will fast for forty days and forty nights. Embodiment means he'll become hungry, tired, and lonely. Satan, the fallen angel, will taunt, tempt, and test him. God from God, One in Being with the Father, he will resist, retort, and return to preach with a new clarity of mind and purpose.

During Lent, we are invited to imitate this sacred vision quest. Our fasting and abstinence officially begins on Ash Wednesday. We, too, may become hungry and tired, but not lonely, because our commitment to Christ means we are never abandoned by God. During Lent we rediscover this truth of our faith. Today, our commitment to self-reflection, soul cleansing, and service to others is evident in the cross of ashes placed on our foreheads.

CELEBRATING AT HOME

In observant Jewish homes, all *hametz* (food made with yeast) is eaten or given away before Passover begins. If you've celebrated Shrove Tuesday according to tradition, all meat, eggs, milk, butter, and cheese would have been consumed during that day's feeding frenzy. Today, as you munch antacid tablets or sprigs of stomach-soothing peppermint, take one last tour through your refrigerator to remove and donate whatever's left.

✝

The ashes you receive at church are made from the palm fronds distributed at last year's Palm Sunday service. The fronds are burned, sprinkled with holy water, and blessed. Celebrating this ritual at church is encouraged but not required. You can—and may—do this at home; indeed, you may have the entire ceremony at home with family or friends. Either follow the Liturgy of the Word using the readings for that day, or simplify the ceremony by focusing on the seasonal blessing of Ash Wednesday. Invite everyone to make the sign of the Cross, then say a few opening words to create a context, and read Psalm 90 or Isaiah 58:5–10.

To create the ashes, remove last year's palm fronds from the cross in your bedroom (see p. 3) and burn them carefully in a well-ventilated place—these blessed palms produce wicked fumes. Next, lightly sprinkle with holy water, and mix ashes with a minuscule bit of oil so they'll stick.

To distribute ashes, use your thumb to make the sign of the Cross as you recite "All come from dust, and to dust all return" (Ecclesiastes 3:20). Or "Turn away from sin and be faithful to the Gospel" (Mark 1:15).

✝

Go fish. Viennese Catholics will dine on herring to mark the beginning of Lent; you can, too. If, however, you really hate herring, you might want to reenact in your own backyard the curious nineteenth-century Lithuanian custom of

Not So Fast!

If fasting is already part of your spiritual practice or something you do regularly as a wellness regimen, then you can probably skip this section. If, however, you're new to fasting or periodically reduce intake because you feel fat, keep reading.

As a spiritual discipline, fasting is intended to be just that—a discipline. Although they didn't articulate it like this, the ancients wisely realized that restricting food and drink was a way to sharpen awareness on many levels. Food fasts, especially rigorous ones, serve to heighten the senses. And because eating is pleasurable, food fasts can indeed induce "suffering."

Lenten fasting is defined as eating only one full meatless meal a day, and two smaller meatless meals that don't add up to another full meal (the Eastern Churches include no alcohol). Never mind that St. John the Baptist allegedly subsisted on a diet of wild locusts and honey, extreme restriction or deprivation will not necessarily make you holier and may, in fact, make you sick. Starving is not fasting.

Nowhere, either in Scripture or church teachings, are we asked to fast at the expense of health and well-being. During the fourth century, St. John Chrysostom wrote, "If your body is not strong enough to continue fasting all day, no wise man will reprove you; for we serve a gentle and merciful Lord who expects nothing of us beyond our strength." The Church in her wisdom exempts those who are ill, younger than fourteen, or older than fifty-nine from fasting. You should also refrain if you've ever been formally diagnosed with an eating disorder, or told you might have one but didn't want to hear it. If this is the case, try fasting from the Internet, daily news reports, or quacking on the phone instead.

dragging a herring around the church. This should, at the very least, be a big hit among the neighborhood cats.

Keep a special Lenten journal for the next forty days. Since the Sacraments of Initiation are celebrated at Easter Vigil (see Chapter 7), you might use this journal to muse about your own preparation for the sacraments, or how the Vespers, Stations of the Cross, and Parish Reconciliation observed during Lent help shape your secular life.

The Big Four-O

Some numbers feature big in the domain of the sacred and their symbolism is obvious; take three, for example. Clearly, this signifies the Holy Trinity, a representation that when multiplied by another sacred three yields nine, the novena number.

Forty is another significant number in scripture and observance. "Lent" is a derivation of the Middle English word Lenten (spring). In Italy it's called Quadrastima, derived from the Latin word *Quadragesima* (forty), the term used by the early Church to refer to forty hours of pre-Easter fasting.

The forty days of Lent are intended to recall Jesus the Christ's forty days of prayer and contemplation in the wilderness before going public. How did he come up with forty? Jewish by birth and education, Jesus knew that biblical periods of holy purgation generally involved either forty days and nights, or years:

> The ancient Israelites escaped Egyptian bondage to wander the desert for forty years before reaching the Promised Land.

Moses fasted for forty days before hiking Mt. Sinai, where he hung out for forty days and nights to receive the Ten Commandments from God.

Moses spent another forty days on Mt. Sinai after the Golden Calf incident.

Jonah gave the city Nineveh forty days to repent. Forty days of prayer, fasting, and contemplation were standard stints for the major Old Testament prophets.

*P*ASSION (PALM) *S*UNDAY

LAST SUNDAY OF LENT

PASSIONTIDE ENDS, HOLY WEEK BEGINS

Developed as a time of remembrance during the first century.

Liturgical color: Red

Jesus enters Jerusalem on a donkey's colt to fulfill Isaiah's prophesy (Isaiah 62:11). His disciples have cushioned his mount with their cloaks. Happy throngs, perhaps including those who have already been miraculously healed, blanket the road to Jerusalem with robes and palm branches.

"Who's this?"

"This is Jesus, the prophet from Nazareth in Galilee" (Matthew 21:1–11).

Lent is over. Jesus has returned from the desert. Holy Week begins.

CELEBRATING AT HOME

Time to remove all signs of spring and life. They will come again in glory, but for now intensify your anticipated joy in the Resurrection—very good news indeed—by removing flowers from your home.

✝

By custom, it's time to cover all statues, crosses, and icons with purple cloth. Think of doing this as a form of fasting, this time from sacred images. Their absence now makes their return on Easter Sunday a more powerful source of joy.

✝

Since the early Church, new converts to the faith have been instructed about the Christian sacraments before and during Lent, then baptized and welcomed into the Church on Easter. For many centuries, catechumens would be taught the Lord's Prayer on Palm Sunday. So what if you've recited this prayer a zillion times, make the Our Father a significant part of today's spiritual discipline. Try:

- Reciting it slowly, so that you're able to feel your mouth shape every word and you have time to truly hear what you're saying.

- Writing it out by hand, so prayer becomes a felt experience.
- Starting over from the beginning every time you catch yourself spacing out.
- Soaking yourself in the sound of any of the beautiful music settings for this prayer.

Note: If you or family members are entering the Church during Easter, give some extra attention to the information in Chapter 7 about preparing for the Sacraments.

> *In* Baptism *and* Confirmation, *the handing on (*traditio*) of the Lord's Prayer signifies new birth into the divine life.*
>
> CCC 2769

In northern and eastern Europe where palms don't grow, pussy willow branches are blessed instead. Even if you have access to palm leaves on Passion Sunday, treat yourself to a huge fuzzy bouquet. (Germans call them "palm kittens." Isn't that adorable?) And this in all likelihood is not true, but Lithuanian folk custom has it that if you comb your hair on Palm Sunday, fleas will grow as big as the buds on those branches.

✝

By now, you've cultivated a lovely group of friends who are totally into expressing devotion through arts and crafts. On Palm Sunday, invite them for an afternoon of palm weaving.

Both social and meditative, this folk art involves braiding

palm fronds into intricate designs that go way beyond the rudimentary crosses anyone fashions by the end of Mass. It doesn't matter if no one is old enough to remember how to do this, you can find easy instructions for making over a dozen different crosses, roses, wreaths, angels, doves, and other Christian symbology by searching for "palm weaving directions" on the Internet.

Serve fresh figs or a fig pie, and you've sustained an old English tradition for what's also known as "Fig Sunday."

✝

Even though they've historically represented fertility (see p. 88), there's probably no way around or out of creating Easter eggs. You could have a real craft-a-thon by decorating hard-boiled eggs along with palm braiding today. This year consider coloring eggs the way early Christians did: red, representing the blood of Christ. Or take it upon yourself to learn any of the Eastern European egg-decorating techniques that use paint, gilding, or wax to create intricate patterns. You can buy a kit, dyes, instructions, tools, design templates, and clean eggshells (duck, goose, ostrich!) from www.surmastore.com.

✝

Perhaps you've seen people's yards decorated with dyed eggs hanging from tree branches and thought, "These folks need to chill out decorating until Christmas." Well, turns out they're observing an old German and Swiss tradition. Originally, brown eggs were stuck onto shrubbery branches to create an Easter Egg Tree. Today you can create the same effect with colorful Styrofoam or plastic eggs that can be reused.

Nervous about the neighbors? Then set up your Easter

Egg Tree indoors; the dog hasn't had any major religious symbols to knock over since December.

Holy Week

Holy Monday . . . . Tossing sinners out from the
Temple of Jerusalem.
Holy Tuesday . . . . Teaching disciples on the
Mount of Olives.
Spy Wednesday . . . . Judas Iscariot decides to
betray Jesus.
Maundy Thursday . . . . The Last Supper. The disciples
conk out at Gethsemane.
Jesus is arrested.
Good Friday . . . . Jesus is crucified, dies, and
is buried.
Holy Saturday . . We watch and wait for the third day,
when Jesus rises in fulfillment
of the Scriptures.

The Paschal Triduum

Before celebrating the Resurrection, we take time to embrace the conflicting emotions of all the events preceding it.

> *Beginning with the Easter Triduum as its source*
> *of light, the new age of the Resurrection fills*
> *the whole liturgical year with its brilliance.*
> *Gradually, on either side of this source, the*
> *year is transfigured by the liturgy. . . . Therefore*
> Easter *is not simply one feast among others, but*
> *the "Feast of Feasts," the "Solemnity of solemni-*
> *ties."*
>
> CCC 1168–9

Holy Thursday

(MAUNDY THURSDAY)
("CLEAN THURSDAY")
SOLEMNITY

Liturgical color: White

It's the great Feast of Passover, a celebration central to Judaism. Throughout his life on earth, Passover in Jerusalem is significant for Jesus the Christ.

Mary and Joseph are frantic when they realize that they're well on their way home from that year's feast without twelve-year-old Jesus. Finding him back at the Temple, they're mystified by his explanation about being in his Father's house (Luke 2:41–50).

Decades later, right before Passover, Jesus will drive merchants and money changers from the great Temple (John 2:13–19). And then, it's time for the Passover seder—one last supper with the disciples, now transformed into the Lord's Supper. Bread and wine become consecrated as body and blood. The Lamb of God is about to be sacrificed, a new covenant made.

The disciples may have fallen asleep at Gethsemane, but we're called to stay awake on *Dies Mandatum*, the day of the new commandment.

CELEBRATING AT HOME

Luke's Gospel tells us that Joseph and Mary brought Jesus to Jerusalem for the annual Passover feast. Had they stayed home in Nazareth, Mary would've been cleaning house. Today's spring-cleaning customs are derived from thousands of years of Jewish Passover preparations. Remember the super-duper cleaning fit you had December 24? Time for another one.

✝

All Gospels report how the Last Supper was a Passover seder, the ritual observance of God's deliverance of the Hebrews from Egyptian bondage. However, because of the way Easter is calculated, the first night of Passover may not line up exactly with Holy Thursday. Nevertheless, you do have several options, each of which will significantly enhance your appreciation of the Triduum:

- Wangle an invitation to a seder at a Jewish friend's home. Don't be shy! Sharing this feast with guests is considered a *mitzvah* (good deed or blessing), so it's unlikely your request will be perceived as rude.
- Attend a community seder sponsored by either a local synagogue or an interfaith organization. Increasingly, church communities are joining with local synagogues to host Passover seders, or are creating ones of their own. My book, *Come to the Table: A Catholic Passover Seder,* will help you create a home or parish-based seder.
- Before going to Holy Thursday services, set aside some time to study the first fifteen chapters of the Book of Exodus. They provide a context for understanding the radical gift of the Holy Eucharist, as well as the radical sacrifice of the Crucifixion.

If you haven't quite gotten around to praying the Sorrowful Mysteries every day during Lent, promise yourself to do so today, at least. Meditating on the Agony at Gethsemane, the Scourging at the Pillar, the Crowning with Thorns, Carrying the Cross, and the Crucifixion will bring a new depth of comprehension and feeling to your Lenten journey.

✝

By custom, meditating on the fourteen Stations of the Cross usually takes place at church on Fridays during Lent. Today, you can intensify your felt sense of awe, gratitude, and humility even more by observing this devotion at home, perhaps lighting a candle, or ringing bells for each station. Try reciting them out loud, with lots of time in between to contemplate each event from the perspectives of:

- Jesus.
- Mary, the *Theotokos*.
- the Apostles as individuals and as a group.
- ordinary disciples.
- the attending mob.
- those who condemned Jesus to death.

Let yourself sink as deeply as you dare—or can bear—into imagining what each felt as:

1. Jesus is condemned to death.
2. Jesus carries His Cross.
3. Jesus falls the first time.
4. Jesus meets his mother, Mary.
5. Simon the Cyrene helps Jesus carry His Cross.
6. Veronica wipes the face of Jesus with her veil.
7. Jesus falls the second time.
8. Jesus speaks to the women.
9. Jesus falls the third time.
10. Jesus is stripped of His garments.
11. Jesus is nailed to the Cross.
12. Jesus dies on the Cross.
13. Jesus is taken down from the Cross.
14. Jesus is buried in the Sepulchre.

Having learned the Lord's Prayer on Palm Sunday, cate-chumens are next taught the Apostles' Creed (see p. 220). Remember how you meditated on the Our Father? Today, focus your attention on the Creed, by:

- Reciting it slowly, so you're able to feel your mouth shape every word and you have time to truly hear what you're saying.
- Writing it out by hand so your profession of faith becomes a felt experience.
- Pondering each sentence as an essential part of your faith as a whole.

✝

The German name for Holy Thursday, *Gründonnerstag*, means "Green Thursday." Green soup made with spinach, parsley, bean sprouts, dill, and cucumber in a chicken or veal stock base; eggs with green sauce; cucumbers and sour cream; and dandelion greens salad are traditional fare in Germany, Austria, and among the Pennsylvania Dutch. Indeed, spring is the general theme across cultures, so feel free to add asparagus or any other green spring vegetable to your Holy Thursday menu.

Good Friday

PASCH (PASSAGE) OF THE CRUCIFIXION
SOLEMNITY

Custom of keeping vigil established during the first century.
Three Hours' Devotion (Seven Last Words of Christ)
    started during the eighteenth century.
Liturgical colors: Red

Jesus is betrayed by Judas. Peter denies knowing, let alone loving and serving him. Pilate succumbs to the raucous crowd and Jesus is hauled away, crowned with thorns. He is forced to carry the cross on which he will hang at the Place of the Skull, Golgotha. Hours later, the Lamb of God will die. Today, we behold all of it from the safe vantage point of our own belief in salvation.

CELEBRATING AT HOME

If you can't or don't attend Good Friday services, you may still capture the somber, quiet, and reflective quality of the day by observing silence between noon and 3 P.M. Use this time to read any of the Gospel accounts of the Passion (Matthew 26–27; Mark 14–15; Luke 22–23; John 13–19).

✝

Wondering when to have hot cross buns? Well, today's the day to indulge in these sweet rolls that are either carved with a cross or inscribed with one in icing. Or perhaps you'd prefer the fifteenth-century German custom of eating big fluffy pretzels with (peeled) hard-boiled eggs? No? Then how about a trip to the barber? Austrian folk tradition has it that a Good Friday haircut will ward off headaches for a year.

*H*OLY *S*ATURDAY

EASTER VIGIL
SOLEMNITY

Liturgical color: White

Jesus the Christ has suffered and died. He is buried.

Having just witnessed superhuman suffering and sacrifice, anything but solemnity seems totally inappropriate. And yet, because we know what will happen on the third day, it's difficult to stifle our gladness as we wait for the Son to rise.

At sunrise on Sunday, our celebration of the Resurrection formally begins but, before then, much happens during the Easter Vigil service. Dark becomes light as the Paschal candle is lit; our own baptism is reflected in the blessing of water; we welcome catechumens into the Church; we're invited to renew our profession of faith; and we return to singing the great Hallelujah with gusto.

> *In his plan for salvation, God ordained that his Son should not only "die for our sins" but should also "taste death" . . . The state of the dead Christ is the mystery of Holy Saturday, when Christ, lying in the tomb, reveals God's great Sabbath rest after the fulfillment of man's salvation, which brings peace to the whole universe.*
>
> CCC 624

CELEBRATING AT HOME

Lent ends at sundown on Holy Thursday, but fasting is often extended until the Resurrection Mass is celebrated. Nevertheless, post-Lenten food preparation generally begins today, concentrating on dishes using ingredients that used to be forbidden during Lent (e.g., eggs, cheese, and meat). Tired of honey-glazed ham and raisin carrot salad? Here's what folks in other countries will eat on Easter Sunday:

GERMANY: Lamb; pickles and mustards; cheeses; *Eier in Senfsosse* (eggs in mustard sauce); fruit and chocolate!

ITALY: Lamb, preferably roasted over an open-air spit; clear broth soup with *pancotta* (fried croutons); an antipasto of cold cuts, pickled fish, and marinated vegetables; garlic-roasted potatoes; platters of sliced tomatoes and artichoke hearts with fresh garlic; salad greens augmented with roasted red peppers; pies made out of cheeses (e.g., ricotta, mozzarella) and sausage or *prosciutto*; fresh fruits (e.g., grapes, pears, figs); ricotta pie; cake flavored with lemon or anise.

EASTERN EUROPE: Roasted pork or pig's head (pigs symbolize good luck); garlicky sausage; jellied meat; baked lamb; baked cheeses; pickled vegetables and vinegary salads; hard-boiled eggs; beet and horseradish relish; *babovka* (poppy seed rings); *syrnyk* (egg and cottage cheese cake); *mazurek* (flat cake covered with nuts, almonds, raisins, and marzipan decorations).

Slavic and Greek families put together food baskets containing anything and everything they'll eat for Easter dinner, then bring them to church to be blessed. As an alternative in keeping with this tradition, contribute Easter dinner foodstuffs to your local food pantry or homeless shelter.

✝

You know that humongous Paschal candle at your church? It's carried into the darkened sanctuary at sundown on Holy Saturday. Its flame, representing eternal life, will be lit during Mass, plus morning and evening prayers until Pentecost and then at every baptism, wedding, and funeral throughout the year. The candle itself represents the "light of Christ rising in glory . . ." (*Lumen Christi*). You may have a Paschal candle—and a new fire-lighting ceremony—at home!

You don't have to get a five-foot pillar, just one big enough to last fifty days. Wonderfully clear instructions for implanting the five grains of incense and for holding a home-based Paschal candle-lighting ceremony are available on www.wf-f.org/HolySaturday.html.

✝

While waiting for the dough for your holiday bread master-pieces to rise, create goody baskets and hide eggs for tomorrow's egg hunt. In addition to chocolates and jelly beans, consider including trinkets that more accurately symbolize the meaning of Easter—little crosses, dove-shaped key rings, scripture cards, or Agnus Dei medals from St. Peter's in Rome.

Maybe start your kids, ones you know, or yourself on a collection of wooden Ukrainian Easter eggs. Swap the bunny for a lamb figurine or plush toy. After all, the Communion Rite does not beseech the *Bunny* of God to have mercy on us.

They Call for Cake? Let Them Eat Bread!

The emphasis on elaborate festive breads at Easter has to do with the fact that the yeast dough rises. Yeast. Rising. Risen Lord. Get it? And, also, eggs were verboten during Lent. Each country has its own golden, sweet, egg-rich version. You *could* buy many of these ready-made, but baking one yourself for the sake of restored tradition is probably worth the effort—at least once! If you don't have a family elder to teach you, look up recipes on the Internet for:

ITALY: *Crescia al formaggio* (cheese brioche); *Pizza Civi-tavecchia* (sweet dough with ricotta, anise, and port or rum); *Pizza Ricresciuta* (sweet dough with ricotta and

cinnamon); *Colomba Pasquale* (sweet dough covered
with crystallized sugar and whole almonds, shaped into
a dove or chick); *gubana* (sweet dough filled with nuts,
dried fruit, spices, and liqueurs); and an egg bread with
whole eggs braided into it.

POLAND: *Baba* or *Babka* (sweet dough with golden
raisins, orange or lemon zest, chopped almonds, candied
orange peel baked in tall round containers).

RUSSIA: *Kulich* (sweet dough with rum raisins and nuts
baked in a clean two-pound coffee can, crown frosted
with confectioners' sugar and decorated with a red rose).

*E*ASTER *S*UNDAY

FIRST SUNDAY AFTER THE FIRST FULL MOON AFTER
THE VERNAL EQUINOX
HOLY DAY OF OBLIGATION

Formally recognized by the Council of Nicea in A.D. 325.
Liturgical color: White

This time, the fragrance of myrrh perfumes the air not of a
manger, but of a tomb. Jesus has been dead for two days and
yet, when the faithful women arrive to sit *shivah* (ritual

mourning) they find an empty tomb. It's the third day, and Jesus has risen in fulfillment of the Scriptures.

Do the women to whom Jesus appears first flee in wordless terror or irrepressible happiness? Jesus, once completely dead, is now fully alive. Death has been conquered, evil vanquished, and scriptural prophecies fulfilled, just as Jesus promised. Imagine his mother's ecstatic relief.

Christ has died. Christ is risen. *Deo gratias!* The road to Emmaus lies ahead, as does the final fish fry, and the Ascension. These are faith events we have not seen and yet we believe, honor, and celebrate. Forty days from now, we'll contemplate Jesus' Ascension into heaven to be seated at the right hand of the Father. Ten days after that, we'll commemorate the birth of the Church when the great Comforter, the Holy Spirit arrived, just as Jesus promised. Today marks Sunday transformed for all time into the Lord's Day for all believers.

> *The Resurrection above all constitutes the confirmation of all Christ's works and teachings. All truths, even those most inaccessible to human reason, find their justification if Christ by his Resurrection has given the definitive proof of his divine authority, which he had promised.*
>
> CCC 651

CELEBRATING AT HOME

If you didn't remove cloth coverings from pictures, statues, and mirrors when you got home from Easter Vigil, do that now! Fill your home with spring flowers—daffodils, tulips, hyacinths, and lilies. Get out the baskets of brightly colored eggs—candy ones included. Set out your best table linens, dishes, flatware, and serving pieces.

One Eastern European tradition to adopt: placing a lamb carved out of butter or formed with sugar at the center of your holiday table, another way to reinforce Jesus as the Lamb of God.

✝

Easter breakfast or Easter dinner? Up to you! In part, this will depend on how you've observed Holy Saturday. Did you attend Easter Vigil as well as Easter Sunday Mass? Were you up at sunrise? Is the extended family coming to your house? Are you responsible for furry friends who need to be walked and fed first thing in the morning, no matter what? Try going with whatever allows you to sustain the wonder of Christ risen. The promise of eternal life does not mean it's okay to kill yourself in the kitchen.

✝

Today would be a superb day to institute—or resurrect if it has fallen by the wayside—the practice of reciting the *Regina Cœli* (Queen of Heaven, Rejoice!) as the customary replacement for the evening *Angelus* of mealtime prayer through Pentecost. According to legend, this traditional Easter season prayer came in 596 to Pope Gregory V, who heard it allegedly sung by angels as he was proceeding through Rome to ward off a plague:

Regina, cœli laetare, Alleluia;
Quia quem meruisti portare, Alleluia;

Resurrexit sicut dixit, Alleluia;
Ora pro nobis Deum, Alleluia.

O Queen of heaven, rejoice! Alleluia!
For the Son you were privileged to bear, Alleluia!
Has risen as He said. Alleluia!
Pray for us to God. Alleluia!

And wait! There's more, added later:

V. Rejoice and be glad, O Virgin Mary, Alleluia.
R. Because the Lord is truly risen, Alleluia.

Let us pray:
O God, who granted joy to the world by the Resurrection of
Your Son, Our Lord Jesus Christ, grant, we beg You,
that through the intercession of the Virgin Mary, His
Mother, we may obtain of the joys of eternal life.
Through the same Christ our Lord. Amen.

(Note: This prayer was yet another Catholic practice that
drove Martin Luther nuts.)

What the Catholic faith believes about Mary is
based on what it believes about Christ, and what
it teaches about Mary illumines in turn its faith
in Christ.

CCC 487

Easter Sunday is only the beginning of an Octave, almost each day of which has at least one custom you might want to celebrate at home.

EASTER MONDAY: Universally reserved for rest, Christians in some countries take an "Emmaus Walk." This leisure activity draws inspiration from the story in Luke, which begins with, "Now that same day two of them were going to a village called Emmaus, about seven miles from Jerusalem. They were talking with each other about everything that had happened" (Luke 24:13–35). Why not get into the habit of taking a ramble (as opposed to a vigorous hike) on this day? As you walk, you might contemplate:

- What it must have been like, back then, to encounter—and not recognize—the risen Christ.
- Times you may have not recognized Christ walking right beside you.

EASTER THURSDAY: Christians in Slavic countries use this day to remember the dearly departed. All Souls' Day observances are equally meaningful during Easter (see p. 125).

EASTER FRIDAY: Traditionally a time of pilgrimage, you might want to visit a special basilica, cathedral, or museum with a noteworthy collection of sacred art. If you have kids, starting this annual excursion when they're young just might mute their future desire to squander spring break in Florida.

True Confessions: Easter

Okay, so we stole most of our Easter stuff from pagans and druids who celebrated the vernal equinox with no shortage of riotous ritual.

The holiday was originally known as Ostra, Ostrara, Ostara, Eostre, and Eastre, all names for the goddess of fertility who awakens dormant earth each spring. Bonfires blazed throughout the night to welcome her at dawn along with song, chant, and dance. Today, we attend sunrise services.

The Easter candle derives from a cultural compromise with the druids. They were not about to give up this form of worship, so St. Patrick created a fire rite to bless the Paschal candle that opens the Easter Vigil liturgy.

Hot cross buns were eaten by Saxon pagans to honor Eostre. Even earlier, ancient Greeks and Egyptians were eating similarly inscribed baked goods during celebrations for Artemis and Isis.

Every ancient pagan culture used eggs to symbolize new life and fertility. Babylonian mythology has the goddess Ishtar (aka Venus) hatching out of a heaven-sent egg. Dyed eggs, totems of rebirth, were traditionally hung in Egyptian temples. Naturally colored eggs, collected from different birds, represented prosperity. The egg hunt was originally a fifteenth-century pretzel search.

Before there was an Easter bunny, there was the sacred hare (*osterhase*). This overgrown rabbit was originally a pagan fertility symbol, for reasons that should be obvious. Sometime during the late seventeenth century, German

Christians had the bunny (who is inexplicably male) delivering eggs. Easter lilies were pre-Christian symbols of fertility, specifically male genitalia. Drenching customs and Baptism hearken back to the pagan (fertility) rite of spring.

Would anyone really mind if we started calling our holy day "Resurrection Sunday"?

Feast Day of the Ascension
FORTY DAYS AFTER EASTER SUNDAY
HOLY DAY OF OBLIGATION

Liturgical color: White

Until the fourth century, the Ascension of Christ into heaven to be seated at the right hand of the Father was celebrated fifty days after Easter Sunday, along with Pentecost. In fact, the entire season was known as Pentecost. Since the seventh century or thereabouts, Ascension has been observed separately, forty days after Easter. In central Europe, one nonliturgical form of celebration involves mountain climbing to commemorate Christ's Ascension from the Mount of Olives. If the prospect of this much exercise gives you the willies (or you live in flatlands), stay home and read the fourteenth and fifteenth chapters from the Gospel of John—after you go to Mass. This is a holy day of obligation.

PENTECOST

(WHITSUNDAY)
FIFTY DAYS AFTER EASTER
FEAST DAY

Concurrent with the Jewish Festival of Weeks (Shavuot).
Became the Christian feast of Pentecost by the second
  century.
Liturgical color: Red

It's Shavuot, and while some observant Jews are spending seven weeks bustling around the great Temple of Jerusalem participating in the *omer* (grain offering and measurement), others are still reeling from everything that has happened since the Crucifixion. Jesus, resurrected from the dead, has appeared to the faithful women and dubious disciples before ascending heavenward in a cloud.

Now they've convened in the upper room to pray and vote in Matthias and replace Judas Iscariot. What's next? Becoming filled with the power of the Holy Spirit on the fiftieth day after Easter. Prophesied by Joel and promised by the Christ, the great Comforter has swept through the upper room with a mighty wind and tongues of fire.

Peter stands before a crowd astonished by the sound of Galileans speaking about God in many different languages.

"Fellow Jews and all of you who live in Jerusalem," he begins, "let me explain . . ." (Acts 1–2). The fellowship of believers increases by thousands. The one, holy, catholic, and apostolic Church is born.

The Spirit will teach us everything, remind us of all that Christ said to us and bear witness to him. The Holy Spirit will lead us into all truth and will glorify Christ. He will prove the world wrong about sin, righteousness, and judgment.

CCC 729

CELEBRATING AT HOME

Now that the decorative wooden eggs are packed away, it's time to get out the dove collection. What dove collection? The one you started around the time you ditched the bunnies and got fixated on lambs.

Medieval churchgoers were treated to the spectacle of a dove figurine, flowers, water, and flaming straw raining down from the church ceiling during Mass. No, you do not have to unseal a skylight or carve a hole in your roof. It would be dramatic enough to reclaim the tradition of hanging carved wooden doves from the ceiling above your dining table for this feast day.

✝

Set your dining table with a red tablecloth and napkins, or use a white tablecloth and scatter it with red rose petals. This custom comes from Italy where red rose petals, representing the flames of holy tongues, were scattered from church ceilings on Whitsunday (*Pascha rosatum*). If you're really feeling flush, spring for a bouquet of fourteen roses, representing the twelve apostles and the two Marys. Accent your décor with red ribbons.

What to eat? Something that used to fly! Cornish game hens are acceptable contemporary substitutes for the doves or pigeons people used to eat to celebrate Pentecost.

The Mary Month of May

Once upon a time and for quite a long time, faithful Catholics would take time for "crowning" ceremonies during May. In fact, the entire month was devoted to maintaining fresh flowers at pictures and statues of the Mother of God. This lovely custom, which seems to have disappeared in some places, is due for a comeback. In *your* home!

At the very least, this would involve crowning a statue of Mary with a wreath of fresh flowers and laying more posies at her feet throughout May. This is especially easy to do with a garden statue of the BVM; another good reason to get one (see p. 233). Another, more elaborate ceremony includes making a big deal of bearing the crown on a cushion, singing the *Regina cœli*, and in a family situation, bestowing the honor of crowning Mary to the oldest or youngest kid. You can find the formal ritual for honoring images of Mary by going to the United States Conference of Catholic Bishops' website: www.usccb.org/publishing/liturgy/mary.html.

Flower Power

Every flower that appears in Christian art is rich with symbolic meaning. Anything involving Mary usually involves any or all of these:

Baby's Breath . . . . Innocence and purity;
                            the power of the Holy Spirit
Blue Columbine . . . . Fidelity
Carnation . . . . Love, life, crucifixion,
                                    "love unto death"
Daisy . . . . Innocence
Gladiolus . . . . Piercing sorrow
Iris (blue) . . . . Fidelity, piercing sorrow;
                            symbol of the Blessed Virgin
Ivy . . . . Faithfulness, eternity
Lily . . . . Purity, humility, obedience
Marigold . . . . Domesticity, simplicity
Rose . . . . Perfect love; Mary herself
Violet . . . . Humility, innocence, constancy
White Columbine . . . . Holy Spirit

CHAPTER FIVE

ORDINARY TIME: SUMMER AND FALL

HERE WE ARE, once again, in Ordinary Time. Keeping true to my promise, I'll repeat that the "Ordinary" in "Ordinary Time" does not mean mundane. Just as winter's Ordinary Time allows us to integrate significant faith events, this period during the summer and fall months provides similar opportunities to live our faith in the afterglow of Pentecost.

For a change, I'm not bothered by the apparent lack of sequence in the holy days. For some reason I have yet to discern, celebrating the Assumption of Mary (August 15) before her birth (September 8) doesn't seem odd. What does snag me a bit is the whole business about when to begin the liturgical year, something I allude to in my pithy observations about the Latin Rite year (see p. 5).

While I've gotten used to changing hymnals and lectionary readings at Advent, I'm not entirely on board for starting the liturgical year then. The Eastern branch of our

Christian family begins the liturgical year with the Birth of the Blessed Virgin. I like that, not just because of its unintended feminism, but because it's closer to the Jewish New Year, Rosh Hashanah. Plus, although many years have passed since I've attended school, summer will always feel like vacation and autumn the start of a new year.

Alas, it doesn't look like the Great Schism is going to be healed anytime soon, so I try to make the most out of this stint of Ordinary Time, which isn't all that hard to do given what's observed during this season. It officially begins the first Sunday after Pentecost and extends through the Feast of St. Andrew on November 30. Whether you share my temporal discomfort or not, you'll see there's no shortage of fabulous feast days to celebrate and a wonderful assortment of customs to revive.

TRINITY SUNDAY

FIRST SUNDAY AFTER PENTECOST
SOLEMNITY

Liturgical color: White

A week has passed since we celebrated the gift of the Holy Spirit at Pentecost. Now we celebrate the fact that our prayers are completed—and truly complete—whenever we proclaim "Glory be to the Father, and to the Son, and to the Holy Spirit."

The magnitude of the Holy Trinity may flicker in and out of focus throughout the year. Maybe today we'll grasp, if only for a moment, the unfathomable, simple complexity of our God.

The mystery of the Most Holy Trinity is the central mystery of Christian faith and life. It is the mystery of God in himself. It is therefore the source of all other mysteries of faith, the light that enlightens them.

CCC 234

CELEBRATING AT HOME

So what if you've spent much of the summer trying to banish all clover from your lawn? Declare a cease-weeding! The three-leaf clover is going to provide your meditative focus.

Yes, the shamrock is a familiar symbol for St. Patrick, the patron saint of Ireland, whose feast day is celebrated March 17. And yes, we're way past March 17. The connection here has to do with an old Irish story about how Patrick used the three-leaf shamrock to explain the mystery of the Holy Trinity to fifth-century catechumens. Here's your meditation du jour:

1. Pick a few shamrocks out of the grass and carefully cradle them in the palm of your hand.

2. Gaze at the three curved leaves, noticing how together they form one unified plant. Take your time, letting your eyes become only one means to see this tiny lesson.

3. Now, gently pluck the leaves from their stem, one leaf at a time, noticing how the shamrock gradually falls apart.

4. Contemplate: What is the shamrock without each leaf?

5. Contemplate: the Father.

6. Contemplate: the Son.

7. Contemplate: the Holy Spirit.

8. Contemplate: What is the Holy Trinity without each person of God?

9. Contemplate: What is each person of God without the Holy Trinity?

Before Plucking That Shamrock . . .

Watch out for attack mermaids on and around Trinity Sunday. This folk superstition comes from Russia, where *rusalki* (mermaids) were said to live in the rivers, streams, and lakes near or within forests.

Legend has it these wraithlike beauties leave their watery lairs on Trinity Sunday or "White Monday" to perch on tree branches. Once up there, they sing hauntingly beautiful songs to entice mortals. If that doesn't work, they'll hop down and launch a sneak attack from behind. These unbaptized souls (sometimes believed to be the spirits of drowned maidens) are determined to *tickle* you to death.

If you believe this, then avoid swimming for the week, or wandering around alone in fields and forests. According to legend, drawing a cross on the ground with a circle around it will protect you, something to keep in mind when venturing forth to gather shamrocks. Don't worry, you'll be able to make up for lost swim time on Assumption Day (August 15).

Corpus Christi

SUNDAY AFTER HOLY TRINITY
SOLEMNITY

Celebrated as a feast during the thirteenth century.
Instituted as a universal feast by Pope Urban IV in the thirteenth century.
Liturgical color: White

The Church already celebrated the institution of the Eucharist on Holy Thursday, but that wasn't enough for a sixteen-year-old Augustinian nun named Juliana, who adored the Blessed Sacrament. For years, she'd had a recurring vision of a full moon, its glowing surface spoiled by a little black spot. What *was* that mysterious blemish? Eventually, Jesus appeared to explain: The moon represented the Church calendar, the black mark the absence of a joyful feast to honor the Eucharist, and he was choosing Juliana to promote what would become known as the Feast of Corpus Christi, the Body of Christ.

By the thirteenth century, this feast had become one of great pomp and circumstance, with community-wide processions and pageants, ringing church bells, marching bands, children costumed in angelic white, and streets decorated with elaborate wreaths of greenery, lilies, and other summer flowers. Corpus Christi always was, and in many countries remains, a public extravaganza. It's a day to celebrate being of, with, and for the Body of Christ.

> . . . by the Eucharistic celebration we already unite ourselves with the heavenly liturgy and anticipate eternal life, when God will be all in all. In brief, the Eucharist is the sum and summary of our faith: "Our way of thinking is attuned to the Eucharist, and the Eucharist in turn confirms our way of thinking."
>
> CCC 1326–7

CELEBRATING AT HOME

Remember those candles you placed in every window during Advent? You can display them for this holy day as well. (This custom is especially popular among Latin American Catholics.) And when your neighbors want to know "what's up with the Christmas candles?" you get to announce that these actually happen to be for Corpus Christi.

Your charming devotional fervor will be appreciated by anyone old enough to remember some of the sweeter aspects of Catholic life, and just might appeal to neighbors who long to enhance their own faith with ritual.

✠

Like carols at Christmas, the traditional hymns for Corpus Christi are well worth depositing in your memory bank. These would be the hymns Pope Urban IV asked St. Thomas Aquinas to compose for this feast. Many Catholics could once sing these by heart; consider restoring them to yours:

Tantum Ergo Sacramentum

Tantum ergo Sacramentum
Veneremur cernui;
Et antiquum documentum

Novo cedat ritui;
Praestet fides supplementum
Sensuum defectui.

Genitori, Genitoque,
Laus et jubilatio,
Salus, honor, virtus quoque

Sit et benedictio;
Procedenti ab utroque
Compar sit laudatio.
Amen.
*(*from Vespers' *Pangue Lingua)*

Down in Adoration Falling

Down in adoration falling,
Lo, the Sacred Host we hail.
Lo, o'er ancient forms departing,
Newer rites of grace prevail;
Faith for all defects supplying
Where the feeble senses fail.

To the everlasting Father,
And the Son who reigns on high,
With the Holy Ghost proceeding
Forth from Each eternally;
Be salvation, honor, blessing,
Might, and endless majesty.
Amen.

O Salutaris Hostia

O salutaris hostia,

Quae caeli pandas ostium,

Bella praemunt hostila;

Da robur, fer auxilium.

(from Lauds' *Verbum Supernum*)

O Saving Host

O Saving Host, O bread of
life,

Thou goal of rest from pain
and strife,

Embattled are we, poor and
weak;

Grant us the strength and help
we seek.

Panis Angelicus

Panis angelicus
Fit panis hominum
Dat panis coelicus figuris
    terminum
O res mirabilis
Manducat Dominum
Pauper, pauper
Servus et humilis;
Pauper, pauper
Servus et humilis.
(from Matins' *Sacris Solemniis*)

The Bread of Angels

The Bread of the Angels
is made the bread of mankind.
Bread given from Heaven,
    terminating all figures.
O marvelous thing!
Nourished on the Lord,
are the poor, the poor,
slaves and the lowly;
the poor, the poor,
slaves and the lowly.

Planting Ahead

Hot, lazy summer days make it difficult, if not impossible,
to imagine the crisp autumn days ahead. Your garden is already blooming, what else could you possibly plant? Well,
have you planted any Aster *novae-anglie*?

More commonly known as the Michaelmas Daisy, this popular perennial comes in white, purple, pink, and blue. It grows and spreads quickly, blooming in time for a freshly picked Michaelmas bouquet on September 29. You can plant this aster variety as late as July.

Assumption of the Virgin Mary into Heaven

AUGUST 15

HOLY DAY OF OBLIGATION

Established by the Eastern Church in the sixth century.
Accepted by the Roman Church in the seventh century.
Declared a dogma of the faith in the twentieth century.
Liturgical color: White

We do not know how, where, or whether Mary experienced bodily death. What we do have is our belief in the resurrection of the dead and in her divinity as *Theotokos*. We have our faith. We have our willingness to swirl in the vortex of mystery when something our Church commemorates fails to make any corporeal sense.

The Assumption of the Blessed Virgin is a singular participation in her Son's Resurrection and an anticipation of the resurrection of other Christians:

> *In giving birth you kept your virginity; in your Dormition you did not leave the world, O Mother of God, but were joined to the source of Life. You conceived the living God and, by your prayers, will deliver our souls from death.*

CCC 966

CELEBRATING AT HOME

Peaches, plums, nectarines, grapes, figs, and tomatoes are now at their luscious best. Those dinky little herbs you planted in June have turned your garden into a fragrant jungle. Behold this abundance and you'll realize why the Assumption of Mary has traditionally been celebrated as a summer harvest holiday.

To make this celebration much more delicious, follow the custom of abstaining from fruit for two weeks before the holy day. Then invite everyone over for a post-Mass feast of fruit soup, fruit salad, fruit juices, and fruit pies. At the very least, adopt the Italian custom of giving fruit baskets to friends and family. Further tradition by decorating your table and home with lilies and roses.

✦

Express your constitutional right to religious freedom by skipping work to hit the beach after Mass on August 15. If anyone asks, explain that you're simply observing "Our Lady's Health Bathing," a venerable custom among Catholics in Ireland, England, and parts of Europe. On this feast day, Mary's blessing extends to natural bodies of water, so taking a dunk in the ocean or a lake, stream, or river is also believed to have salutary benefits. Sorry, but the Jacuzzi at your local day spa does not count, even if you get a Dead Sea salt scrub with organic loofah mitts beforehand.

More Good News about Assumption Day!

According to superstition, life is particularly peachy for thirty days after Assumption Day. Until September 15, you can count on peacefully coexisting with nature. You will not be attacked by wild animals or be bitten by snakes. Poisonous plants will be harmless. Whatever food you pick will be super-salubrious. Alas, no guarantees are made about your neighbor's pit bull. Nor is it clear that Mary's munificence extends to any exotic produce you purchase during Our Lady's Thirty Days.

THE BIRTH OF THE BLESSED VIRGIN MARY

SEPTEMBER 8

FEAST DAY

Established by the Eastern Church in the fifth century.
Adopted by the Roman Church in the seventh century.
Liturgical color: White

Hail Mary, full of grace! The Orthodox Church calls her *Theotokos*—the one who gave birth to God. Today, we celebrate her birthday, not that we know all that much about it. After all, the infant Mary and her parents, Anne and Joachim, are never mentioned in Scripture. What we do have is a tale from the second-century apocryphal Book of James (aka the *Protevangelium*).

The circumstances surrounding Mary's birth remind us of God's promise to Sarah and Abraham in Genesis (Genesis 18:10–15). You know that story. They're old; she's barren. Sarah laughs out loud when she overhears God telling Abraham she'll bear a child in her dotage. Later she'll laugh with amazed joy when Isaac is born. This time, the aging, childless Joachim heads off to the desert for forty days of fasting and prayer while the aging, childless Anne sits home in the garden and prays, "Oh God, remember Sarah? You blessed her with Isaac. I beg you to bless me, too." An angel appears to explain that these prayers have already been answered. "I will dedicate this child to God," promises Anne.

Does she have even a clue about her daughter's divine destiny? Well, we do! And so we celebrate the Birth of the Blessed Virgin Mary, *Theotokos*, light-bearer, whose unqualified "yes" made the Incarnation possible in her son and our Lord, Jesus the Christ (see The Annuciation of the Lord, p. 51).

What the Catholic faith believes about Mary is based on what it believes about Christ, and what it teaches about Mary illumines in turn its faith in Christ.

CCC 487

CELEBRATING AT HOME

Consider renouncing your adolescent vow to never ever have a Mary lawn ornament like your crazy aunts. You're absolutely right—life-sized statues of the Blessed Virgin Mother with floodlights are more suitable for church courtyards. Instead, what you need is a small, lovely statue of the BVM to nestle sweetly among some flowering vines. This being September, you're likely to find one on sale at a local garden store. Take time to contemplate all the options and you'll know exactly which Mary statue to bring home.

It'll be the one that whispers to your spirit, "I'm right here."

✝

Who doesn't enjoy a birthday party? This is a feast day, so invite friends over for cake. White, of course, festooned with white and blue icing. Party favors? Roses. Silk ones—they'll have everlasting life. Instead of singing "Happy Birthday to You," sing the *Regina Cœli* (see pp. 85–86) or recite this prayer from Matins of the Divine Office:

> *Lord God,*
> *the day of our salvation dawned*
> *when the Blessed Virgin gave birth to your Son.*
> *As we celebrate her nativity*
> *grant us your grace and your peace.*
> *Through Christ our Lord,*
> *Amen.*

Even though St. Anne shares a memorial day with St. Joachim on July 26, her faithfulness provides a fine focus for meditation. Indeed, which prayers of yours have already been answered without your knowing it? If you keep a prayer journal, check the entries for December of last year and make a note to check your calendar nine months from now in June.

✝

In October we'll celebrate the Our Lady of the Rosary, so start putting out the word that you're hosting a rosary-beading party.

St. Michael and the Archangels Gabriel and Raphael

(MICHAELMAS)
SEPTEMBER 29
FEAST DAY

Established by the Roman Church in the fifth century to
celebrate St. Michael the Archangel.
A holy day of obligation until the eighteenth century.
Archangels Gabriel and Raphael included during the
twentieth century.
Liturgical color: White

Angels are appointed messengers of God, and St. Michael the
Archangel is considered the most powerful among them. The
Eastern Church, in fact, regards Archangel Michael "Who is
like God" as Prince of the Seraphim, the angel closest to God.

As the angel who stopped Abraham from sacrificing
Isaac, the angel through whom God handed the Ten Commandments to Moses, and the angel who fought Satan for
the body of Moses, Archangel Michael is the guardian of Israel as well as "Defender of the Catholic Church."

Archangel Michael reigns supreme among angelic warriors; charged with rescuing souls from evil, and leading the principalities and powers into battle against Satan—something to ponder the next time you invoke "the powers that be."

Finally, St. Michael escorts all souls to eternity. The old funeral liturgy included this prayer: "May the standard-bearer Michael conduct the departed into the holy light which was promised to Abraham and his seed." Is it any wonder that his name means "Who is like God" and he's the first angel to rate a feast day? Now behold the two glorious spirits with whom he shares it.

Archangel Gabriel, "Hero of God," or "Strength of God," appears throughout Scripture, petitioning God to part the Red Sea, informing the prophet Daniel when the Babylonian exile of the ancient Israelites would end. In the New Testament, he announces the birth of St. John the Baptist to Zechariah and greets Mary with the news that she has been blessed among women to bear the Christ. According to legend, Archangel Gabriel will herald the second coming of Christ with a trumpet.

Archangel Raphael "God has Healed" appears only in the Book of Tobit. As divine medic, Archangel Raphael restored sight to Tobit, is said to have visited Abraham after his circumcision, and healed the world after it was defiled by the sins of fallen angels.

As revealed in Scripture, these fiercely protective celestial beings far surpass anything we could possibly create in art or imagination. Today we give them special thanks for their invisible yet holy tangible presence in our lives.

*. . . the whole life of the Church benefits from
the mysterious and powerful help of angels.*
CCC 334

Celebrating at Home

For centuries, St. Michael's Day was celebrated with great feasts. Among the English, Celts, and Scots this meant tucking into a roasted goose fattened on corn and barley, harvest leftovers. Sixteenth-century landlords usually received a goose along with rent payments on the quarter-day of Michaelmas. You, however, will probably need to place a special order with a butcher, although first check in the freezer section next to ducks.

Rub the inside cavity with salt, the outside with salt and pepper; stuff it with a bread dressing seasoned with sage and onion to absorb the fat. Geese are even fattier than ducks, so roast yours on a rack and pierce the skin well with a sharp fork so the fat can drain during cooking. Figure thirty minutes per pound in an oven preheated to 350°F and allow thirty minutes of stand time.

Goose is a very rich game bird, so keep accompaniments relatively light, although you must include carrots! Everyone—because you'll be inviting lots of people to this feast—will want to have room for dessert. What's for dessert? Angel food cake. The traditional St. Michael's bannock is a breadlike cake more appropriate for breakfast.

Eat a goose on Michaelmas Day, you'll never want for money all the year round.
ENGLISH PROVERB

In Scotland, carrots feature big at the Michaelmas feast. In the Hebrides, women and girls harvest wild carrots, then tie them together with red thread to form bouquets. Michaelmas guests receive these carrot bouquets as gifts. This custom might charm children—and veggie-resistant adults—into eating this orange root. Given the health benefits of carrots, which are especially good for improving eyesight, feel free to point out how St. Raphael would approve.

✝

Oh, so you *do* want to make St. Michael's bannock for breakfast? It's easy and takes about an hour, start to finish. While the oven is preheating to 375°F, mix together 2 cups flour, 2 tablespoons sugar, ½ teaspoon baking powder, ½ teaspoon baking soda, and ¼ teaspoon salt. Cut in 2 tablespoons butter (not margarine), then add 1 cup of buttermilk or yogurt to make a soft dough. Toss in a handful (or two) of currants or raisins. On a floured surface, knead the dough until smooth, then pat into an 8-inch round loaf and bake for 40 minutes on a greased cookie sheet. To get the full festive effect, score the dough with crosses. Cool on a cookie rack. For optimal pleasure, serve warm with butter and jam.

✝

As you petition any or all of the archangels, lighting candles will help you memorize their special prayers. Each archangel can be represented by a white candle, but let the spirit move you to use any of their other symbolic colors. For St. Michael, orange or gold. For St. Gabriel, silver or blue. For St. Raphael, yellow or gray.

✝

The Michaelmas daisy plants you've tended all summer are flowering. Go out and cut yourself a bunch.

Prayer to St. Michael

> Saint Michael, Archangel, defend us in battle.
> Be our defense against the wickedness and snares of the
>   Devil.
> May God rebuke him;
> We humbly pray; and thou, O Prince of the Heavenly
>   Host,
> by the power of God,
> thrust into hell Satan and all the other evil spirits
> who prowl about the world for the ruin of souls.
>   Amen.

A Prayer to St. Gabriel

> Blessed Saint Gabriel, Archangel,
> we pray that you intercede for us at the throne of divine
>   mercy:
> As you announced the mystery of the Incarnation to
>   Mary,

so through your prayers
may we receive faith and courage,
find favor with God,
and redemption through Christ our Lord.
May we sing the praise of God our Savior
with all the angels and saints in heaven
forever and ever. Amen.

A Prayer to St. Raphael

Blessed Saint Raphael, Archangel,
we pray that you help us in all our needs and through
    life's trials
as you, through the power of God, restored sight and
    gave guidance to Tobit.
We humbly seek your help and intercession,
that our souls may be healed,
our bodies protected from all sickness,
and that through divine grace we may become fit
to dwell in the eternal Glory of God in heaven. Amen.

The Good News about Angels

You may believe in and celebrate the unseen presence of these immortal spirits without apology. Angels are in the Bible, and belief in them is a salvific requirement! However, this does *not* mean you have to inundate your home with cheesy cherub figurines.

Angels

Ranking Orders and Marching Orders
(Medieval theologians came up with this
chart of angelology)

THE FIRST TRIAD

Closest to God's Throne
Seraphim—Continually sing God's praises
Cherubim—Worship God
Thrones—Oversee justice in Heaven

THE SECOND TRIAD

Guard Heaven and Earth
Dominions—Assign duties to other angels
Virtues—Work miracles
Powers—Protect us from evil

THE THIRD TRIAD

Earth Duty
Principalities—Protect nations and cities
Archangels—Deliver messages from God
Angels—Guard us personally

THE GUARDIAN ANGELS

OCTOBER 2

FEAST DAY

Introduced in Spain during the sixteenth century.
Extended to the universal Church in 1670.
Liturgical color: White

Didn't we just celebrate the archangels? Yes, we did. Three days ago, to be precise. Today we focus specifically on guardian angels, those spirits charged with ministering over us as individuals.

"That there is an angel for each one of the faithful no one will contradict," declared St. Basil who, among other Church fathers, was fairly emphatic about angels existing.

Some people believe guardian angels are assigned at Baptism, but this is not a Church teaching. Most everyone agrees, however, that we were assigned at least one guardian angel at conception. These angels are commissioned by God to protect us from evil, harm, and temptation. Let's thank them.

From its beginning until death, human life is surrounded by their [angels'] watchful care and intercession. "Beside each believer stands an angel as protector and shepherd leading him to life." Already here on earth the Christian life shares by faith in the blessed company of angels.

CCC 336

CELEBRATING AT HOME

On the theory that it's never too late to have a happy childhood—or to help create one—take time to learn or teach these classic prayers:

Child's Prayer to the Guardian Angel

> *Angel of God, my guardian dear,*
> *to whom His love commits me here,*
> *ever this day be at my side,*
> *to light and guard, to rule and guide. Amen.*

Prayer to the Guardian Angel

> *Angel sent by God to guide me,*
> *be my light and walk beside me;*
> *be my guardian and protect me;*
> *on the paths of life direct me.*

Why not create an elegantly lettered version of this prayer to frame and hang in your bedroom? If you don't know calligraphy, play around with the fancy fonts that come with your word processing program—maybe letting each family member create a customized version.

✝

There probably isn't any angel food cake left over from September 29, but if there is, go ahead and finish it with great ceremony right now.

OUR LADY OF THE ROSARY

OCTOBER 7

FEAST DAY

Pope Gregory XIII established the Feast of the Holy Rosary in the sixteenth century.

Became Our Lady of the Rosary and extended to the universal Church in the seventeenth century.

Liturgical color: White

Every major religious tradition has a special vocal prayer practice to help the restless mind surrender more fully to God. For Catholics, it's praying the Rosary. Your (great?)

grandmother, especially if she was an immigrant to the United States, probably prayed the Rosary daily. You undoubtedly received a set—or three—of rosary beads at key sacramental moments in your own life.

If praying the Rosary hasn't been a feature of your regular prayer practice, use this feast day to get started. Since the entire month of October is dedicated to the Rosary, you have plenty of time to get back—or leap forward—into this devotional groove. Throughout the year, we'll have abundant opportunities to zoom in on either the Joyful, Sorrowful, Glorious, or the Luminous Mysteries. For more details about praying the Rosary, see Appendix B.

> *In celebrating this annual cycle of the mysteries of Christ, Holy Church honors the Blessed Mary, Mother of God, with a special love. She is inseparably linked with the saving work of her Son. In her the Church admires and exalts the most excellent fruit of redemption and joyfully contemplates, as in a faultless image, that which she herself desires and hopes wholly to be.*
>
> CCC 1172

CELEBRATING AT HOME

Observe the Feast of Our Lady of the Rosary by hosting a get-together to make rosaries. You can find most of the supplies at a bead store, or perhaps a Catholic bookstore. For each rosary, you'll need:

53 small beads
 6 large beads
59 eye pins (heavy enough to withstand a lot of
     handling)
 3 small jump rings
 1 8-inch chain of base metal, silver or gold

Pick up round nose pliers if you don't already own a pair. You may have to go to a religious supplies store to buy a crucifix and a Miraculous Medal centerpiece.

If you're an experienced beader, you'll look at the supplies and exclaim, "Wow! Why didn't I ever think of doing this before?" If it's all new to you, the friendly store proprietor—because all beading store proprietors are very friendly—will show you how to twist eye rings so they'll link together without kinking. You can also find detailed rosary instructions by logging on to www.rosary parts.com.

(Note: Plastic beads work well for kids, as does having them make a smaller wrist rosary that has one decade of Hail Mary beads and one Our Father bead.)

Count It All Joy

Generally, it's much more economical to buy semiprecious stones on strands rather than individually. In either case, choose beads by handling them as if you were already praying.

Crystals might catch your eye, but notice if you find the edges irritating to touch repeatedly. Keep in mind that wooden beads will absorb body oils.

Close your eyes. Can you distinguish between the larger and smaller beads? Take your time. Let selecting beads become a contemplative exercise in and of it itself.

All Hallows Eve

(HALLOWEEN)
OCTOBER 31

Celtic New Year rituals merged with All Saints' Day observances during the ninth century. Originally known as Allhallowmas, then All Hallows Eve, then Hallowe'en.

Liturgical color: White

Many believe Halloween is an exclusively pagan holiday having absolutely nothing to do with Christianity. Not so! Although Halloween has been secularized since the nineteenth century, Catholics have a long history of observing evening vigil before the Feast of All Saints. Put in this context, Halloween shifts from being a commercial holiday to All Hallows Eve, a commemorative holy day.

CELEBRATING AT HOME

What may seem like a treat for adults can be tricky for parents with children in the thrall of popular culture. You'll need to start educating and encouraging them young, if you want kids to dress up as angels instead of devils. Hosting an annual costume shindig with other families automatically gives you more control over party content and tone. So will sending invitations noting that your Halloween party celebrates the Vigil of All Saints' Day.

✝

Emphasize Christian generosity and the tradition of Catholic social justice by encouraging your children to "trick or treat for UNICEF" (United Nations Children's Fund). For over fifty years, UNICEF has encouraged children to collect pennies on Halloween to enhance the quality of life for the world's underprivileged children. Have issues with UNICEF? Then collecting money for Mercy Corps (www.mercycorps.org) or Catholic Relief Services (www.catholicrelief.org) is a perfectly wonderful substitute.

✝

No kids? No problem! You can do your bit to offset the commercial weirdness of Halloween by donating to one of the children's relief organizations on your own. You probably can't get away with throwing prayer cards or little crosses into trick-or-treat bags, but you can offer a silent prayer along with candy.

All Saints' Day

(HALLOWMAS)
NOVEMBER 1
HOLY DAY OF OBLIGATION

Established as a universal feast by the Roman Church in
the fourth century as the Feast of All Martyrs.
Extended to celebrate All Saints' during the eighth century.
Became a holy day of obligation during the ninth century.
Liturgical color: White

Throughout the year, we recognize extraordinary women and men who established the early Church, many of whom sacrificed life and limb in the process. And yet for every martyr (witness) we know about, there are thousands upon thousands whose names we'll never know—people plucked out of their homes, silenced in schools, and banished to prison even today. They, too, are saints who shape our faith. Over the centuries, they've been slaughtered for inviting others to believe in God's love evident and incarnate, Jesus the Christ. They're our cloud of witnesses. Today, on this holy day of reflection, we're theirs.

Exactly as Christian communion among our fellow pilgrims brings us closer to Christ, so our communion with the saints joins us to Christ. . . .

CCC 957

CELEBRATING AT HOME

Sustain the reverential impact of All Saints' Day by listening to any, or a few, of the world's most beautiful requiem (funeral) masses composed by Brahms, Fauré, Mozart, Schubert, or Verdi. Aim for prayerful listening, letting the music become both the subject and source of contemplation.

✝

Pretzels? Yes, pretzels. Usually regarded as a traditional food for Lent, in some Eastern European countries, pretzel making is also an All Saints' Day ritual. The dough for these pretzels is shaped into a figure eight, to represent saints or martyrs.

Unless you enjoy making bread from scratch, skip this labor-intensive step and use prepared bread dough from the supermarket. On a lightly floured surface, roll dough into ropes about 12 inches long. Twist each rope into an eight. Place these "saints" on a greased baking sheet 1½ inches apart, then brush with an egg white beaten with water. Sprinkle with coarse salt. Bake 15 to 20 minutes, or until golden in an oven preheated to 375°F.

✝

Even if you already set aside a day to celebrate the saint whose name is linked to yours, this is another good day to meditate on "your" saint's extraordinary life of faith.

Tomorrow, we'll commemorate friends and family who have died. Tonight, on the eve of All Souls' Day, light a candle for each person you're memorializing. And in the spirit of All Saints' Day, light an extra candle to represent all unnamed martyrs.

To Die For . . .

To die for. Not to be a cranky literalist, but . . . really? This bit of hyperbole, which entered American slang during the 1970s, refers to something extraordinarily desirable. For early Christian martyrs, religious conviction was indeed something to die for and the promise of eternal life with God helped ameliorate the agony. But we don't have to reach back to antiquity for models of sanctity. Recent history provides many heinous examples of those murdered because of their faith. On this holy day of All Saints especially, take a few minutes to contemplate the full meaning of this idiom. What cherished beliefs are *you* willing to die for?

*A*LL *S*OULS' *D*AY

NOVEMBER 2

FEAST DAY

First celebrated during the tenth century.
Put on the Roman calendar during the thirteenth century.
Liturgical color: White or violet

Yesterday we prayed specifically for martyrs. Today we'll pray for all members of our faith community. Although we'll focus primarily on those we've personally known and loved, our prayers extend to all believers—living and dead.

We pray for those who have died in faith. We pray a speedy transition for those whose heaven-bound transport may be running a bit late. We pray for "poor souls" who don't have anyone to pray for them. On this day, solemnity and joy coexist as we remember those we miss, yet celebrate their journey home to God.

> *Our prayer for them [the dead] is capable not only of helping them, but also of making their intercession for us effective.*
>
> CCC 958

CELEBRATING AT HOME

Throughout the world, the Day of the Dead is observed with festivities ranging from relatively somber, to over-the-top ecstatic. After all, the faithful departed get to spend eternal life with God. What's not to celebrate? Embrace or modify any of the following customs. All involve remembering with food, flowers, and candlelight, both at home and graveside.

> **Food:** For centuries, European families prepared a feast on the evening of November 1 to share with the dear departed. The dining table included a place setting, complete with favorite foods, for the dead soul; windows and doors were left open to allow easy entrance.

A Lithuanian Prayer for All Souls
(nineteenth century)

Dear souls of the dead,
you are still remembered by my family,
you are most worthy of our perpetual remembrance,
especially you, my grandparents, parents,
also our relatives, children, and everyone death took away
    from our home.
I invite you to this annual feast.
We pray that this feast be agreeable to you,
just like the memory of you is to us.
Amen.

Mexican Catholics hold exuberant picnics in cemeteries to celebrate *Dia de Muertos* (Day of the Dead). Preparation may
start as early as October 30. In addition to the departed's favorite foods, traditional dishes like spicy chicken *mole, pan
de muertos* (bread of the dead), and *leche quemada* (milk
candy) are served. Everyone exchanges, and snacks on, sugar
skulls with the deceased's name written on the forehead in
icing. In some Mexican communities, including those in
the southwestern United States, mariachi bands serenade.

What happens with the leftovers of these fabulous repasts?
Whatever isn't eaten by the living relatives is usually do-
nated to those in need. You can build on this custom by
donating food or funds to your community food pantry as
a memorial gift. Instead of waiting until December, consider making your annual memorial contributions to med-
ical education, assistance, and research foundations now.

Flowers: Bouquets or wreaths of seasonal flowers such as
chrysanthemums, marigolds, and asters, or grave blankets
of evergreens are traditionally used to decorate cemetery
plots. In some predominately Catholic countries, the entire month of November is dedicated to graveside repair,
maintenance, and beautification.

Candles: Candles at home and hundreds of votive candles
at graveside are traditionally lit to help all souls find
their way home to God. (Note: Check with the cemetery caretaker before lighting graveside candles.)

Home Altars: Mexican families traditionally build elaborate *ofrendas* (altars of the dead), sometimes trans-
forming an entire room with flowers, incense, photos
of the deceased, toys for *los angelitos* (souls of children), candles, fruits, vegetables, statues of saints, and

favorite foods and beverages. Carved wooden skulls, symbolizing death and rebirth, are also placed on the altar, which is draped with lace or other fine cloth.

Make All Souls' Day a time to haul out photo albums and tell stories, with reverence and delight, about friends and family no longer with us.

Should Catholics Celebrate Thanksgiving?

Some people think Thanksgiving originated with the Puritans, but it was a Pilgrim thing. Most people consider them interchangeable groups, and although they were not, neither Pilgrims nor Puritans were big fans of Catholics. Both groups of Protestant settlers despised Catholicism for its ornate liturgical piety and ecclesiastical structures.

The Pilgrims, who believed the Church of England was also beyond redemption, sailed over on the *Mayflower* and ended up settling in Plymouth, Massachusetts. Governor William Bradford might have thanked almighty God for sending Squanto and getting everyone through their first harsh winter, but the Pilgrims never considered this a religious holiday. Indeed, whenever these devout folk observed "thanksgivings," they fasted and prayed.

So if all this is true, why should Catholics bother celebrating this secular holiday? I'll give you two reasons, one grounded in history; the other grounded in our Catholic faith.

First, Protestants weren't the only ones exiting Merrie Olde England. The English Catholics who arrived at Clement's Island on March 25, 1634, founded Maryland. (Mary, Mother of God. Land. Maryland. Get it?) When they landed, Father Andrew White, S.J., celebrated a Mass of Thanksgiving. And although we don't know this for sure, it's likely they had some kind of feast after this Eucharistic celebration. But even if they didn't leave that first Mass and tuck into a pile of soft-shell crabs, they certainly celebrated thanksgiving in the truest sense of the word—as do we *every* time we come to the table of the Lord.

"Eucharist" comes from the Greek word meaning "to give thanks." At every Mass, we remember that on the night Jesus was betrayed, he took bread and gave God thanks and praise. And because celebrating the Eucharist is at the center of our sacramental faith, daily Mass is daily Thanksgiving. Paying extra special attention to this on the fourth Thursday of November is another way of being the little "c" catholics we're called to be as capital "c" Catholics.

*F*EAST OF *C*HRIST THE *K*ING

LAST SUNDAY IN ORDINARY TIME
SOLEMNITY

Established in 1925 by Pope Pius XI
Liturgical color: White

Being a relatively new addition to the liturgical calendar, this devotional feast hasn't given rise to any notable home-based customs. Maybe you'd like to start one to reinforce the kingship of Jesus as Christ and Our Lord. I'm thinking it's time to reprise the King's Cake you baked on Shrove Tuesday.

ST. ANDREW, THE FIRST APOSTLE

NOVEMBER 30

FEAST DAY

(MARKING THE END OF ORDINARY TIME—SOMETIMES!)

Born: B.C.E.

Died: C.E. 60

Liturgical color: Red

Andrew snapped to attention when Jesus passed by. John the Baptist exclaimed, "Behold, the Lamb of God," and Andrew immediately wandered off. After spending a day with Jesus, Andrew announced to his brother Simon Peter, "We have found the Messiah!" (John 1:41).

Still, it would be a while before Andrew devoted his life to the Christ. The call ultimately came in a metaphor. As he walked along the Sea of Galilee, Jesus saw Andrew and his brother fishing. "Come, follow me," he said, "and I will make you fishers of men" (Matthew 4:19).

What else do we know about this saint the Greeks call the *Protoclete* (First Called)? It was Andrew who pointed out the five small barley loaves and two little fishies that would end up feeding a crowd of five thousand. Andrew preached the Gospel in Greece (and perhaps what was Russia) before being crucified on an decussate (X-shaped) cross.

His place on the liturgical calendar provides an important marker. In a few days, we'll be fished out of our ordinary lives. Advent begins the first Sunday after this feast. For four weeks, we'll marvel at Mary's abundant willingness and wait with joy for the birth of Our Lord, Jesus the Christ.

CELEBRATING AT HOME

In Scotland, which claims St. Andrew as its patron, the whole day will be one of celebration. You can join in the spirit by baking scones which—get this—are made just like St. Michael's bannock (p. 111). Boost the sugar up to ¼ cup and use a large biscuit cutter to cut the dough into circles. This time, slice an X in the top of each scone to represent the cross on which St. Andrew was crucified.

✝

A German folk tradition has children going door to door to collect gifts or donations for charity. Instead of wandering the neighborhood, donate your time, energy, and talent to a community-based soup kitchen or food pantry to honor St. Andrew's role in finding food for the hungry multitudes.

✝

St. Andrew is also the patron saint of marriage and fertility. Need you read more?

CHAPTER SIX

$\mathscr{D}$AILY $\mathscr{D}$EVOTIONS

$\mathscr{E}$VERY DAY PROVIDES myriad opportunities to create a home—and life—in the image and likeness of faith. While you may need to modify these opportunities to fit contemporary demands, you certainly don't have to reinvent them. The daily Bible readings that constitute the Liturgy of the Word provide a logical foundation for home-based devotions. The Church provides a structure for this and prayer in the Divine Office (aka Liturgy of the Hours).

> *The Liturgy of the Hours is intended to become the prayer of the whole People of God. . . . The laity . . . are encouraged to recite the divine office, either with the priests, or among themselves, or even individually.*
>
> CCC 1175

DEVOTIONS AT HOME

Specific daily readings are cataloged in the Divine Office, a compendium also known as the "Breviary," although you'll discover how it has nothing to do with brevity. You could haul around four hefty volumes with more ribbons than a maypole, but why? Daily readings are available on any number of Catholic websites (see Appendix E). Your church's weekly bulletin probably lists them as well. You can then look them up in any Bible.

Hours of Hours

Centuries ago, if you lived in a strict religious community, you'd be praying with other exhausted monks or nuns every three hours. Over time, the Divine Office has been modified to reflect changes in consecrated life. Today, although the Office can be recited privately, monastic communities still come together to recite:

Morning Prayer (Lauds)
Daytime Prayer (Middle Hour, combining what used to be Prime, Terce, Sext, and None)
Evening Prayer (Vespers or Evensong)
Night Prayer (Compline)

Visit a retreat house if you want the glorious experience of bells and responsorial chanting throughout the day.

The Divine Office includes hymns, canticles, psalms, reflections, and intercessions along with Scripture readings. Secular reality being what it is, you probably don't have the time for such devotional fervor. That's okay. Focus specifically on the Office of Readings at your convenience. Your immortal soul is not imperiled if you read all, or only some, of the readings first thing in the morning or before you conk out at night.

✛

Regularity and continuity support prayerfulness, so schedule your Scripture reading for the same time (or times) each day when you are,

- Better able to focus on devotions without distractions.
- Clear enough to comprehend what you're reading.
- Relaxed enough to meditate on the reading.

Depending on time demands,

- Collect all reading citations for the entire week, marking your Bible ahead of time so you can easily find them.
- Make finding the daily readings part of your spiritual practice the evening before or first thing in the morning.
- Subscribe to a monthly missal (e.g., *Magnificat*) that has everything you need in one place.

Be realistic about the time you can devote to reading deeply. Better to do this wholeheartedly one day a week than overcommitting to a rigorous schedule of readings. Start slowly to develop both a taste and hunger for daily devotions.

> *In Sacred Scripture, the Church constantly finds her nourishment and her strength.*
>
> CCC 104

If you can focus on Scripture only one day a week, you may as well choose Sunday! The Lord's Day is a holy day of obligation, and observing a day of rest is one of the top Ten Commandments. So, why not spend part of your Sabbath contemplating at least the Mass readings you just heard and maybe peeking ahead to readings for the coming week?

> *The institution of the Lord's Day helps everyone enjoy adequate rest and leisure to cultivate their familial, cultural, social, and religious lives. On Sundays and other holy days of obligation, the faithful are to refrain from engaging in work or activities that hinder the worship owed to God, the joy proper to the Lord's Day, the performance of the works of mercy, and the appropriate relaxation of mind and body.*
>
> CCC 2184, 2185

If the prospect of "praying Scripture" seems daunting, then zoom in on psalms, which are already songs of praise, thanksgiving, and the like. You could probably spend an entire lifetime praying with the Psalms!

✛

Collect various translations of the Bible, perhaps using different ones for different types of reading. For some people, the Psalms and Gospels will always read best in the lyrically beautiful and completely archaic *King James* (Anglican) version. For others, words like "thou," "hast," and "verily" obscure what the text means. The *New Jerusalem Bible* and the *New American Bible* are popular among Catholics, as is the Revised Standard Version Catholic Edition, which has been approved by the Vatican for liturgical use. Take a look at these and other translations and use whichever translation touches your mind, heart, and soul.

One "must have" translation for Old Testament readings is *Tanakh: The Holy Scriptures: The New JPS Translation According to the Traditional Hebrew Text* (The Jewish Publication Society, Philadelphia: Pennsylvania, 1985).

> *The Old Testament is an indispensable part of Sacred Scripture. Its books are divinely inspired and retain a permanent value, for the Old Covenant has never been revoked.*
>
> CCC 121

It'll be easier to adopt the habit of regular Scripture reading if you have Bibles at home. Note the plural usage, which implies having more than one Bible for:

Catholics and the Bible

Christian faith is anchored in both the Old Testament (Hebrew Scripture) and New Testament (Christian Scripture). Taken as a whole, these histories, prophecies, parables, poems, proverbs, and letters document our relationship to God and reveal God's message to us. The Bible is the central text of faith, read throughout the year as the Liturgy of the Word.

Like many Christian denominations, we read *all* Scripture with reference to Jesus Christ as the incarnate revelation of God's love. Unlike some, we believe the Bible is a text *inspired by God* and *written by humans* who lived during ancient times.

- Reference and display (e.g., opened on a book stand for walk-by readings).
- Notes and highlighting for future inspiration.
- Comparing different translations.
- Tucking into your briefcase, purse, backpack, or car's glove compartment.

As you read, experiment with:

- Reading silently, taking time to meditate on a word or phrase in the prayer tradition of *lectio divina.*
- Making like a lector and reading out loud to yourself or your household.
- Instead of reciting the Psalms, chanting them in plainsong or singing a contemporary Psalm setting.

- Standing or sitting as you read, noticing how the words "feel" as you change your posture.
- Sketching the images that come to mind, heart, and soul as you read.

Make time to memorize passages that move you, keeping in mind that memorization is commonly known as learning something "by heart." At some point, when you collide with life, whatever you've stashed away in memory will emerge to serve you. Memorization techniques include:

- Writing out the passage a zillion times.
- Reading the passage out loud a zillion times.
- Creating a tape to play a zillion times.

In addition to formal prayers, structure your day to include quality time talking with and listening to God. Again, it's okay to accommodate realities of contemporary life. God will be perfectly pleased to accept your prayers.

- Written out in a prayer journal, diary, or on the back of your food shopping list.
- While you're driving, brushing your teeth, or reading the newspaper.
- If you're half asleep at the beginning or end of the day.
- When they're as short as "thank you" or "help."
- Spoken in slang.
- In silence, from your heart.

> *Whether we realize it or not, prayer is the encounter of God's thirst with ours. God thirsts that we may thirst for him.*
>
> CCC 2560

Latin Rite Catholics are rediscovering the power of praying with icons. Note that it's praying "with" not "to" icons. These exquisite paintings of Jesus, the Holy Mother of God, the saints, and angels have long been a liturgical feature for Eastern Christians.

Prayer in this instance is silent and involves gently, steadily beholding the image. Already deeply meditative, this prayer form can become more so when you focus on your breathing as you gaze at the sacred image.

You can easily find hand-painted icons or reproductions online or in religious gift shops, but consider learning how to paint one. You actually do not have to have *any* artistic talent at all. The process involves tracing traditional images and using the canon of color. (You don't get to decide that Mary would look prettier in pink.) All you need is the wholehearted willingness to be in prayer. To learn how to paint icons using contemporary acrylic medium, look at workshops offered by iconographer Peter Pearson (www.nb.net/~pearson/). If you'd like to explore traditional egg tempera techniques, check out the Prosopon School of Iconography (www.prosoponschool.org).

Christian iconography expresses in images the same Gospel message that Scripture communicates by words. Image and word illuminate each other.

CCC 1160

Keeping a Prayer Journal

Maybe you've been taught not to pester God with specifics. Well, here's what Jesus Christ has to say about *that* in the Gospel according to Mark: "Whatever you ask for in prayer, believe that you shall receive it, and it will be yours" (Mark 11:24).

Even if you already believe that every prayer is answered, keeping a prayer journal will help you track divine reality. You may keep this along with your regular journal of thoughts, feelings, and dreams, or separately. In any event, create a space to write out prayer requests. You can either do this in the form of a letter or by simply listing your heart's desire—peace within my family, safe travel for my friend, comfort for all those who mourn, a Maltese puppy. Remember to date entries so you can fully appreciate how and when your prayers are answered.

By the way, the answer to your prayers won't always come in the form of "yes." You may not like the answer "no" or "not quite now," but it's still an answer. And always the right one.

Launch family devotions at the beginning, or end, of the day, doing any or all of the following:

- Lighting a candle and praying for others (intercessions).
- Reading the Psalms, readings, and Gospel *du jour.*
- Learning more about the saint *du jour.*
- Praying the Lord's Prayer.
- Praying the Profession of Faith.
- Praying the Rosary (see Appendix B).

In our own time, in a world often alien and even hostile to faith, believing families are of primary importance as centers of living, radiant faith. For this reason, the Second Vatican Council, using an ancient expression, calls the family the Ecclesia domestica *(domestic church).*

CCC 1656

Morning Prayer

O Jesus,
through the Immaculate Heart of Mary,
I offer you the prayers, works, joys, and sufferings of this day.

ST. FRANCIS DE SALES

Yes, there are countless numbers of established, well-known prayers. But that shouldn't stop you from crafting and writing out your own prayer. This might also be a great family project, or something that a group of friends could create to celebrate a special occasion or even something routine, like food shopping! Any cry from the heart to God counts as prayer. The cry from *your* heart is *your* prayer.

✝

Consider praying the Rosary at home with a group of faithful friends. Whoever leads announces the Mystery to be contemplated before each decade. Everyone prays quietly in unison. You can deepen the experience even more by having someone read out loud relevant biblical passages for each Mystery, or perhaps by discussing what meditating has revealed.

Start by getting together once a week to conquer initial discomfort of praying in such an intimate environment. Gather together on different days until each set of Mysteries has become embedded in your awareness. (See Appendix B for more details about the Rosary.)

> *In Hebrew, amen comes from the same root as the word "believe." This root expresses solidity, trustworthiness, faithfulness. And so we can understand why "Amen" may express both God's faithfulness toward us and our trust in him.*
>
> CCC 1062

Establish a tradition of Compline (Night Prayer) for yourself or your family that includes the following:

- Reviewing and assessing the day's events in light of your faith and trust in God (i.e., an Examination of Conscience or Penitential Rite) in writing (see Appendix D for the Confiteor).
- Offering the day's actions up to God.
- Prayers for protection throughout the coming night.
- Good-night kisses.

Enhance your prayer with any of these traditional physical expressions of devotion, supplication, or adoration:

- Kneeling at the side of your bed or before your family altar.
- Standing with great poise and dignity.
- Raising your hands, palms heavenward.
- Prostrating yourself, flat out and downward on the floor.
- Folding your hands, palms together.
- Holding your hands forward, fingertips touching.

Try incorporating these gestures into your private prayers. The kinesthetic action of moving your body will serve to keep you aware of what you're doing.

According to Scripture, it is the heart *that prays. If our heart is far from God, the words of prayer are in vain.*

CCC 2562

You, too, may institute the Great Silence at your house! This is the blissful quiet that descends in monasteries after Compline, generally by 9:30 P.M. Imagine what your interior experience would be like without the external distractions of television, telephones, tunes, and your own nattering at the dog.

Night Prayer

Protect us, Lord, as we stay awake;
watch over us as we sleep,
that awake, we may keep watch with Christ,
and asleep, rest in his peace.

TRADITIONAL

And what goes on between the prayerful endpoints of the day? Blessings, of course! It's never too late—even if you're being held hostage by teenagers—to introduce the spiritual habit of saying "grace" before meals. Thanking God for sustenance can be traced to earliest biblical times. To put this practice in context, take a tour through the Five Books of Moses (Genesis, Exodus, Leviticus, Numbers, Deuteronomy) and the Gospels (Matthew, Mark, Luke, John), noting all instances where God is thanked and food is blessed before it's eaten.

✝

Start the tradition of saying grace before meals, rotating the honor among all members. What? Your family is too busy to partake of a family meal? Then start the tradition of a family meal! And turn off the TV while you're eating it.

Aw, Do We Hafta?

Once upon a time, when parents were in charge, children didn't dare question whether their attendance at family devotions was necessary. If they did, "yes" meant "be there or else." Children may have gotten huffy back then, but parents won the battle for authority; no lives lost and lots of character built.

Alas, times have changed drastically, and parents are being sued or shot by children for less. But not in your house! To ensure that your kids want nothing more than to obey the Fourth Commandment, engage them in family devotions when they're very young—*in utero*, if possible.

What? They're *whining*? Well, although Jesus was not talking about child-rearing practices, he may as well have been when he said, "Simply let your 'Yes' be 'Yes,' and your 'No,' 'No'; anything beyond this comes from the evil one" (Matthew 5:37).

If you say grace and no one's around to hear it, do you make a sound? Yes. Practice thanking God before meals, even if you're eating alone; even if it seems downright weird to do so at first.

Worried about spooking guests by saying grace? Ah, here's something to "think" rather than "feel" through. Consider the possibility that guests might be inspired, honored, and touched by seeing you (and your family) start a meal by giving thanks. Notice whether your discomfort is on their behalf or your own.

Grace 101

Gee, someone *else* always said grace. Now it's your turn and you haven't a clue how to do it. As everyone looks expectantly in your direction, you feel struck dumb *and* stupid. You know that "Rub-a-dub-dub, thanks for the grub, yay God!" just ain't gonna fly, but what to do or say?

Start by focusing on the primary reason for saying grace and the primary feeling it's supposed to evoke—gratitude. That would be gratitude for having food to eat, a place to eat it, and enough to share with others. Feeling grateful will help you express gratitude, so corral your thoughts and feelings in that direction. Notice also whether this is a special time on the liturgical calendar or a special season for those at your table. These details will help you craft a blessing.

Invite everyone to hold hands. Touch reinforces connectedness.

What to say? Start by thanking God. End by saying "Amen." Don't stress over what you say in the middle. Stick with the classics until leading grace ceases to freak you out:

> *Bless us, O Lord, and these, thy gifts, which we are about to receive from thy bounty, through Christ our Lord. Amen.*

> *For this our daily food, and for every gift that comes from you, O God, we bless your holy name through Jesus Christ our Lord. Amen.*

Finish up by making the sign of the cross. (Release hands, first.) Not everyone at the table is Christian? Use this and skip the hand signals:

> *Blessed are you, Lord God, ruler of the universe; you give us food from the earth. Amen.*

After a while, you'll be relaxed enough to add details like asking God to "bless this food you have made and human hands have prepared," or thanking God "for the privilege and delight of sharing a meal with friends."

Quick. Think. Without flapping your hands, how would you teach someone to make the sign of the "large" cross? Here's how: (in the name of the Father) Move the right hand from the forehead to the chest, (and to the Son) to the left shoulder, (and to the Holy Spirit) then to the right shoulder, and then back to the heart (Amen). Which fingers? Latin Rite Catholics use two fingers (forefinger and middle finger, or forefinger and thumb). Yes, there's a "small" cross. It's made by tracing the sign of the cross with the thumb on the forehead, lips, and heart. It's used during Mass before the Gospel reading.

> *The Christian begins his day, his prayers, and his activities with the Sign of the Cross: "in the name of the Father and of the Son and of the Holy*

Spirit. Amen." . . . The sign of the cross strength-
ens us in temptations and difficulties.

CCC 2157

Blessings are sacramentals that bring liturgical life to the home front. You don't have to wait until Epiphany or before Lent to bless your house. You don't have to wait until the Feast of St. Francis of Assisi to bless your kid's gerbil. Nor do you have to wait for the parish priest to show up to bless guests, flowers, fruit baskets, or vacation travels. As a baptized Christian, you may bless just about anything you want by:

> Praising and thanking God for the person, place, thing, or situation.
> Invoking in the name of Jesus Christ and making the sign of the cross as you bless a person, place, thing, or situation.

You may simply speak the blessing and read appropriate Scripture. You may also use holy water, perfumed oil, and incense, if you'd like. In fact, it wasn't that long ago that most Catholics kept a bottle of holy water at home for private blessings, prayers, and ceremonies. Get yours from your parish church.

Sacramentals derive from the baptismal priest-
hood; every baptized person is called to be a
"blessing," and to bless.

CCC 1669

*D*EVOTIONAL *R*EMINDERS

There's a reason why Catholic churches usually have exquisite stained-glass windows, life-sized statues, bas-relief panels recalling Stations of the Cross, flowers, and other ornamentation. There's a reason for glorious music and liturgical chant. Beautiful sights and sounds lift the spirit in ways words do not.

Just as daily devotions will serve to enhance your spiritual life and Catholic identity, so too will filling your living space with sensory reminders of faith. What would your home look like if you decorated it to reflect God's glory, mercy, and love through Jesus Christ? How much more happy and peaceful would you feel if at least part of your home reminded everyone of a retreat center?

Sacred images in our churches and homes are intended to awaken and nourish our faith in the mystery of Christ. Through the icon of Christ and his works of salvation, it is he whom we adore. Through sacred images of the holy Mother of God, of the angels and of the saints, we venerate the persons represented.

CCC 1192

DEVOTIONAL REMINDERS AT HOME

It's time to resurrect the home altar tradition. And if you're inclined to go on a tear about the First Commandment, please take (yet another) tour of your home.

What's hanging on your walls or from your windows? Native American dream catchers because they're charming? Crystals because they're pretty? Do your kids venerate rock stars on slick posters? Does Barbie's outfit get changed to reflect the seasons? See that electronic box everyone gathers around for hours, all eyes glazed over with adoration? What's on the kitchen bulletin board or pasted to the bathroom mirror? Flip through your kid's sticker book (or yours!) and notice the images. Now, what were you going to say about idol worship?

✝

Keeping in mind that your family altar will be a focal point for devotions throughout the liturgical year, set it up where it's accessible yet protected. Choose a place conducive to prayer and meditation, using a table large enough to hold any or all of the following:

- Candles.
- An open Bible, missal, or prayer book.
- A cross or Crucifix.
- Icons or statues of Jesus, the Blessed Virgin Mother, angels, or patron saints.
- Framed Scripture quotes.
- Incense burner.
- Flowers.
- Family pictures or memorabilia.

Candle Stash

Whether or not your parish priest observes the custom of blessing candles at Candlemas (February 2), you'll still want to lay in a stock of candles for various commemorative and celebratory occasions—holy days, holidays, mealtimes, and, of course, prayers. Prayer candles range from little votives that accompany prayers of petition to relatively large vigil candles (e.g., Novena pillars that last for nine days of continuous burning) that symbolize prayerful waiting.

At home, you get to be the Altar Society. Just think—no uncharitable bickering with the biddy who wants to use candlesticks you hate. You may rearrange stuff as often as you'd like:

- Using the appropriate liturgical colors and different fabrics for each special occasion (e.g., brocades, velvet, lace).
- Adding symbols and images to commemorate saints' days.
- Coordinating fresh or silk flowers to symbolize the season.
- Decorating the altar thematically (e.g., celebrating the Rosary in October, celebrating Mary in May, Feast Days for patron saints, anniversaries).
- Rotating the responsibility for altar decorating and upkeep among family members.

Color Me Sacred

COLOR IN RELIGIOUS SYMBOLISM

White: Purity; joy and glory.

Red: Fire and blood; martyrdom.

Blue: Heaven; truth.

Green: Nature; hope of eternal life.

Purple: Sorrow; suffering.

Black: Death; mourning.

VESTMENT COLORS

Advent and Lent: Violet representing purification or penance.

Christmas, Paschal Triduum, Easter, Holy Days, Feast Days: White representing joy and triumph.

Special Feast Days and Holy Days: Red representing fire, martyrdom, and royalty.

Ordinary Time: Green representing growth and life.

Observant Jews affix a *mezuzah* to the doorways of their homes. This little box, which is touched reverently upon entering and leaving, contains a piece of parchment inscribed with Deuteronomy 6:4–9; 11:13–21. It reminds all who pass by it about the eternal presence—and blessings—of God. In Catholic homes, a holy water font by the front door could serve a similar function in addition to recalling baptism (see Chapter 7). Blessing self and others with holy water and the sign of the cross is a powerful reminder of a commitment to live a Christian life.

Even if you don't want to add a font to your foyer décor,

you might nevertheless get into the habit of offering a blessing as you (and family) head off to work, school, or errands.

✝

As your home comes into visual alignment with your faith,
you might next ask what, in God's holy name, is that racket
blasting forth from the stereo? Bona fide scientific research has
revealed the health benefits of listening to, if not actually participating in, liturgical chant. You can significantly boost your
endorphins and simmer down your adrenaline by playing this
and other sacred music in the background as you go about
daily business. Check out Gregorian chants recorded by Chan-
ticleer and the Benedictine Monks of Santo Domingo de Silos
or medieval chant and polyphony recorded by Anonymous 4
and Sequentia. (For more music suggestions, see Appendix E.)

✝

Ever notice how much of the Mass is surrounded by hymns?
There's no reason why you can't sing these at home! You will
make your church's choir director very very happy by learning
tunes and words *before* showing up at church, and then actually
singing along—whether or not you're officially in the choir.

✝

Crucifix or cross? Consider displaying both images in your
home. Your spiritual needs, preferences, and sources of inspiration will change over time.

Which Crucifix? One that depicts Christ as suffering
servant with whom we stand, trusting God's redeeming
love? The Crucifix representing Christ the King, crowned
with light and clothed in glory from the cross?

Which cross? The Latin cross representing the cross on which Jesus was crucified? (✝) The Jerusalem or Five-Fold Cross representing the wounds of Christ? (✚) The Celtic cross whose circle represents eternity? (☦) The Pointed Cross or Cross of Suffering? (✝)

Which Crucifix or cross? Choose the one or ones that help you begin to comprehend the tremendous suffering, love, and triumph of God through Our Lord, Jesus the Christ.

The Great Commission

It's a dark and stormy night when your doorbell rings and there, on your front porch, are two earnest young people dressed like grown-ups and toting knapsacks filled with religious tracts. Go ahead—invite them in for a chat!

Why?

Because at the end of the Gospel According to Matthew, you will find these words red-lettered: "Therefore go and make disciples of all nations, baptizing them in the name of the Father and of the Son and of the Holy Spirit, and teaching them to obey everything I have commanded you" (28:19–20).

Because you can probably bet they're not Catholic and know next to nothing accurate about Catholicism—Latin or any other Rite.

Because you have probably never been taught how to talk about your Christian faith or your Catholic practices and could use the practice.

Because your visitors are missionaries and *they* could use the practice!

Because God is giving you a great opportunity to teach, learn, and rely on the Holy Spirit for words and wisdom beyond your mortal capabilities.

Start by asking lots of questions. This process will help you clarify, and possibly articulate, what you believe. At the very least, you may be inspired to read the *Catechism of the Catholic Church* or show up for religious education classes. Offer your visitors a seat, a beverage, and your attention. For a fun and instructive time, ask:

- What goes on during a typical service at your church?
- How do you pray?
- How often do you receive Communion?
- What do you believe about Communion?
- Who has divine authority in your church? How is that authority bestowed or conveyed?
- What you do believe about Scripture?
- What do you believe happens after death?
- Is Mary the Mother of God? If not, whose mother is she?
- How do you define sin?
- How are our sins forgiven? Does your church teach that there's anything specific to do?
- Do you have statues and artwork in your church? If not, why not?
- Do you believe in heaven and hell?
- How do you celebrate the Resurrection of Christ?
- What happens if you marry outside your church?
- What do you think Catholics believe?

• What would you like to ask me about Catholicism?

And if no missionaries ever show up on your doorstep, use these questions to help you articulate what you believe the next time you encounter someone with an inquiring mind and heart.

CHAPTER SEVEN

*H*ONORING THE *S*ACRAMENTS

*A*T THE VERY BEGINNING of Church history—certainly during the first century—almost all sacramental celebration took place at home. It had to; there were no churches! But even when, for example, the Eucharist was celebrated at a home-based meal, it was not restricted to family members. Holy Communion was shared with other believers; this sharing served to reinforce faith and community. Holy Communion and the other six sacraments (as affirmed by the Council of Trent in A.D. 1547) are conferred and celebrated within the embrace of Christian community. They, in turn, serve to create and shape that community which today gathers not at home, but at a church.

The sacraments are radically social—shared in and by community. Maybe we don't always love our neighbors as much as our professed faith demands. Maybe we flat out don't like the people sitting next to us at church. We judge the competence of those new parents at the baptismal font and question someone's choice of spouse. Perhaps we've been extremely lax in attending Parish Reconciliation. But when we celebrate the sacraments, we celebrate—and demonstrate—our commitment to live with others as Christians "in the unity of the Holy Spirit."

While the sacraments are church-based celebrations supported by church-based catechesis, there is much that family and friends can do on the home front. The "domestic church" must also play a key role in extending the grace of each sacrament in daily life. Here you'll find traditions and suggestions for doing this. Over time, you may create additional ways to live a more grace-inspired life by asking:

- What is the essential nature or grace of this sacrament?
- How can I prepare at home to receive this sacrament at church?
- What home-based activities will support this sacrament after I've celebrated it at church?

The Sacraments

These seven sacraments of the Catholic Church allow the faithful to experience and share in God's grace. Each one draws us into a deeper, more personal, and ultimately more loving relationship with God the Creator, Christ the Redeemer, and with the Holy Spirit the Divine Counselor.

Sacraments of Christian Initiation
    Baptism
    Confirmation
    Eucharist

Sacraments of Healing
    Reconciliation and Penance
    Anointing of the Sick
Sacraments of Vocation/Service
    Holy Matrimony
    Holy Orders

The sacraments of Christian initiation—Baptism, Confirmation, and the Eucharist—lay the foundations of every Christian life. . . . The faithful are born anew by Baptism, strengthened by the sacrament of Confirmation, and receive in the Eucharist the food of eternal life.

CCC 1212

*T*HE *S*ACRAMENTS OF *C*HRISTIAN *I*NITIATION

BAPTISM

Unto you, or someone, a child is born—and then what?

In Catholic families, infants are welcomed into Christian community through the sacrament of initiation known as Baptism. Membership in the Body of Christ begins—and happens once for all time—through this sacrament, which may also be conferred upon adult converts. If you're committed to raising your child in the Catholic faith, then plan on preparing for and participating in this sacrament.

Early on, the faithful would troop adult initiates to the nearest body of water on Holy Saturday. Once there, they'd be completely submerged three times—in the name of the Father, the Son, and the Holy Spirit. Next, they'd be anointed with charism (holy oil) and adorned in white garments (that they'd wear for fifty days) before being whisked off, now squeaky clean of sin, to celebrate their First Eucharist.

Now, you'd think, given our great love of ritual, Catholics would always insist on baptism by full immersion, but that's not what has evolved over time. Depending on your perspective, you'll be either dismayed or relieved to know that sprinkling (aspersion) or pouring (infusion) rites at the church baptismal font have replaced this older ritual in many parishes. And, nowadays, as a general practice, only adult catechumens get to experience the spiritual trifecta of Baptism, Confirmation, and First Eucharist during Easter Vigil. Everyone else, which is to say, babies and children under the "age of reason" (seven, amazingly), are baptized into the Catholic faith during a special ceremony either at or after Sunday Mass.

Actually, you *could* request full immersion, although it might be nerve-wracking to watch your newborn get dunked underwater. Plus, since *any* baptized Christian has the right and privilege to baptize another, you technically don't need a priest to perform this rite in an emergency. But before you indulge your vision of a backyard pool party with your tennis partner officiating, remember that consecrating a new life to Christ is a community event. This, like all other sacraments, derives and confers meaning when celebrated in public.

Under certain special situations, like when a newborn's life is in jeopardy, an on-the-spot baptism is permitted. The Catholic Church has a ceremony, minus the actual Baptism (because "we acknowledge one Baptism . . ."), when the baby is well enough to be in public. Normally, Baptism is scheduled any time from a few weeks to a few months after birth so that the mommy can be present without keeling over and extended family members can attend. But even if out-of-towners can't make it, be assured that your parish community is there to pledge their help in raising your child. Sorry, but this does not mean your pew mates are available to babysit. It means that they're committed to providing a prayerful, spiritual context for religious formation.

No matter what the circumstances, you're always welcome to have a more exclusive party afterward for family and friends. You're under absolutely no ecclesiastical obligation to serve brunch to your entire parish, although kicking in for parish coffee and cake is a nice gesture of gratitude.

Preparing at Home

Your church probably offers baptismal preparation classes. In fact, your parish probably requires you to be a registered parishioner *and* attend these sessions before your baby may be baptized. During these sessions, you'll learn more about what the rite means and involves. Contact your parish about its baptismal preparation requirements at least three months before your baby is born. Plan to attend baptismal preparation while your baby is still swimming around *in utero* and everything is still relatively quiet.

✝

Continue preparing for Baptism at home by contemplating:

- How baptismal promises have shaped your spiritual and secular life, especially your life as a parent.
- The meaning you hope Baptism will have for your child over the years.
- Your relationship with your parish community and what it could become.
- What it means to truly raise a child "in the faith."
- Placing fresh flowers on the BVM (see pp. 92 and 93).

> *Holy Baptism is the basis of the whole Christian life, the gateway to life in the Spirit (*vitae spiritualis ianua*), and the door which gives access to the other sacraments.*
>
> CCC 1213

Preparation time also lends itself to reading Scripture about Baptism in the life of Christ and his early disciples. You might want to contemplate what these passages imply about the relationship between Baptism and Christian life. Take a look at:

Matthew 3:11–17; 28:18–20
Mark 1:9–11
Luke 3:5–16
John 3:1–8
Acts 1:4–6
Romans 6:1–5
1 Corinthians 12:12–13
Galatians 3:26–29
Ephesians 4:1–6

The Baptismal Profession of Faith
(APOSTLES' CREED)

I believe in God, the Father almighty,
        creator of Heaven and Earth.
I believe in Jesus Christ, his only Son, our Lord.
            He was conceived by the power of the Holy Spirit
                and born of the Virgin Mary.
            He suffered under Pontius Pilate,
                was crucified, died, and was buried.
            He descended to the dead.
            On the third day he rose again.
            He ascended into heaven,
                and is seated at the right hand of the Father.
            He will come again to judge the living and the dead.
I believe in the Holy Spirit,
        the holy catholic Church,

> the communion of saints,
> the forgiveness of sins,
> the resurrection of the body,
> and the life everlasting. Amen.

As long as you're studying Scripture, you may as well behold what Jesus the Christ had to say about children in Mark 10:13–16.

✝

In addition to being witnessed by community, Baptism also involves the witnesses or godparents of your choice. The Church, of course, would prefer that you come up with a godmother and a godfather, but one godparent will do just fine—as long as she or he is a Catholic at least sixteen years old and has received all the Sacraments of Initiation. Remember, too, the godparent vows to play an important role in your child's spiritual formation. Keeping all these criteria in mind, pick someone who takes Catholicism seriously enough to:

- Embrace not only doctrine, but Catholic sacraments, traditions, and customs.
- Participate actively in parish life.
- Represent the Christian community and model how Christian faith is lived in daily life.
- Attend baptismal preparation classes.
- Be present at significant sacramental events throughout your child's life.

- Participate in your child's religious education.
- Wrap your child in prayer.
- Remember the kid's "Baptismday" every year.

Note: Many of these criteria will also apply to choosing a sponsor at Confirmation.

✝

Oh dear, you had planned to ask your favorite uncle, the one who ditched Catholicism for another church, to be your child's godparent. Well, according to Canon Law, he can't be the godfather, but may act as a Christian witness *if* you find a practicing Catholic to act as godmother. And it doesn't matter how much you love her, forget about asking the cousin who became a Theravadan Buddhist. She doesn't believe in baptism. How's she going to wholeheartedly transmit Catholic faith and its practices?

✝

Here's something to figure out in the privacy of your own home: your child's name. Ever wonder how the Catholic kids always ended up with names like Theresa or John? Well, it's because there has yet to be a St. Lindsay or St. Brad.

While the Church no longer *requires* you to name your baby after a canonized saint, you might want to do so anyway. For one thing, having endured over time, saints' names will remain tolerable. (Honestly, can you picture a Tiffany with liver spots? I didn't think so.) More important, naming your child after a saint automatically provides a patron, an exemplar, and yet another special day to celebrate God's goodness and grace.

However, the Church does insist that you avoid any

name that's clearly anti-Christian—on the extremely re-
mote possibility that you were going to name your child
Ananias or Sapphira.

Note: You may use the same name at Confirmation. In
fact, doing so reinforces the link between these sacraments.

✛

Traditional Baptism garb is white—for your child, that is.
This represents "putting on Christ." Sometimes the church
provides a white robe or stole to be used during the ceremony and kept afterward to commemorate the occasion. If
your family doesn't already have an heirloom christening
gown, here are two other traditions to consider:

> Fashioning baptismal robes out of the same cloth that was
> used to create the mother's wedding gown or train.
> Assigning godparents the traditional honor of providing
> the christening gown.

Note: You'll be dressing your baby at home and will not
have to undress the tyke for the rite, but do bring a towel
and a change of clothes if you're opting for full immersion.

✛

You'll be leaving this ceremony with a candle, in addition to a
baptized and, if you're lucky, a quiet baby. During the ceremony this taper is lit from the large Easter candle to symbolize your child's freedom from darkness by the Light of Christ.
Hang on to this candle! It'll play a feature role in home-based
celebrations for many years, if you're careful not to burn it too

long at any one celebration and store it in your freezer. As your kid gets older, you can use this candle as a foundation for teaching what it means to share the Light of Christ.

✝

Don't lose the paperwork! You'll need that Baptismal Certificate for just about everything in the life to come—CCD registration, First Communion, Confirmation, Marriage, and heaven forefend, Annulment. Add it to the pile of other important documents you have stashed in the family safe. No family safe? Uh-oh. You'd better go get one or sign up for a safe-deposit box at your local bank.

You're the Mommy

Another birth-related rite that seems to have disappeared is what was once known as the Churching of Women. This church-based ritual, which is often assumed to be post-birthing purification, is generally cited as yet more evidence of Church misogyny. Consider, though, how such a ceremony might be seen as a way to *honor* new mothers. If you think this proposition is a stretch that could leave marks, behold the opening two verses of Psalm 121. The entire psalm was part of the rite as early as the eleventh century and may be a source of comfort, especially if you have a fussy newborn:

I lift my eyes to the hills—
   from where does my help come?
My help comes from the Lord,
   the maker of Heaven and Earth.

✠

Haul out the family Bible—if it's not displayed on or near the family altar as suggested in Chapter 6—and record the baptismal date. If you don't already have this information recorded, you may as well note sacramental anniversary dates for everyone else in your family.

You may also want to invoke all of Psalm 121 as you plan the post-Baptism party. This is hosted at home, and if it's at yours, keep it simple and put someone else in charge of setup and cleanup. This might be just the honor to bestow on the friends whom you love but didn't canonically qualify as godparents.

✠

By custom, your christening party menu should be dominated by white, light, and sweet foods. Decorate with white flowers, balloons, and more candles. Scallop shells are also used to symbolize Baptism, even though they were originally pagan fertility symbols. Did you string little white lights during Christmas? Well, you can use them again for this party. Bring out the dove collection you displayed for Easter and Pentecost! Put out a baby book and ask guests to write a little something about your child's Baptism or perhaps their own. Siblings involved? Maybe they could be persuaded to compose a special poem, craft a banner, or have pictures of their own Baptisms displayed.

The party parameters for Confirmation are basically the same with one major exception: The Confirmation candidate is no longer a baby and may participate in party planning (e.g., addressing invitations), then help extend hospitality (e.g., welcoming and serving guests).

You're a Guest

You didn't have the baby. No one asked you to be an official witness. You're an honored guest! You're wondering, "What am I supposed to be doing?" Well, at the church, you're *not* supposed to be jumping up on the pews or scrambling around the baptismal font with a video camera. Save that for the house party.

Your next big question is undoubtedly, "Should I bring a gift?" Here's the scoop on gifts for the Sacraments of Initiation (Baptism, Confirmation, First Eucharist). If you're invited, but don't attend, you're not expected to send something. May the Holy Spirit guide you to a greeting card that doesn't make you gag.

If you're invited and attend, depending on your closeness to the family, your gift may range from a bouquet of flowers to a monetary gift in the child's name (e.g., savings bond, stock, charitable contribution). If you're Catholic, it's appropriate to give sacramentals and items like religious jewelry, saint statues, saint medals, guardian angel figurines, children's books, or icons. If you're Christian, but not Catholic, don't give stuff you'd never use in your own faith practice (e.g., a rosary). If you're neither Catholic nor Christian, then you really are quite the honored guest! How about giving the *parents* a gift certificate to a restaurant or the movies? At some point, they'll need a break from parenting fun.

CONFIRMATION

How and when Confirmation is celebrated may have changed over the centuries, but the "why" of this Sacrament of Initiation has not. At different points in history, this special anointing either has occurred before or after First Eucharist; during childhood, adolescence, or adulthood; was performed by either the bishop or his emissary. Despite these fluctuations, Confirmation has always been a time to renew baptismal vows and to "seal" the candidate with the gift of the Holy Spirit. Like baptism, this sacrament involves parish participation. Witnessing this rite, the entire community remembers, renews, and rejoices in its own commitment to Christian life.

While many home-based Confirmation activities are *similar* to those for baptism, they are not the *same*. Here's why: In the United States, most Latin Rite confirmands are preadolescents. They're old enough to know—and question—what it means to be confirmed in the Catholic Church. Now, more than ever, the family's involvement in sacramental preparation takes on greater meaning and has the potential to exert both positive and negative influence. No pressure, parents, but this may be your last chance to instill a reverence and delight for Catholic Christianity in your kid.

> Like Baptism which it completes, Confirmation is given only once, for it too imprints on the soul an indelible spiritual mark, the "character," which

is the sign that Jesus Christ has marked a Chris-
tian with the seal of his Spirit by clothing him
with power from on high so that he may be his
witness.

CCC 1304

Rite of Confirmation

All powerful God, Father of our Lord Jesus Christ,
by water and the Holy Spirit
you freed your sons and daughters from sin
and gave them new life.
Send your Holy Spirit upon them
to be their helper and guide.
Give them the spirit of wisdom and understanding,
the spirit of right judgment and courage,
the spirit of knowledge and reverence.
Fill them with the spirit of wonder and awe
in your presence.

PREPARING AT HOME

The Rite of Confirmation invokes the seven gifts of the
Spirit named by the prophet Isaiah. What does it mean
to be "sealed with the gift of the Holy Spirit"? The
Confirmation class is going to discuss this at length and
your preteen will have homework along these lines. Prepare for the conversation by considering this question
yourself: "How has the sacrament of Confirmation shaped

the quality and direction of my life?" Try to gently, skill-fully weave this inquiry into dinner conversation or a car talk.

Just because your preteens are considered old enough doesn't mean they are mature enough for Confirmation. Since this sacrament is also about choosing to become a member of the Catholic community, it's probably worth waiting to take the classes until the Confirmation candidate (your child or you):

- Wants to receive this sacrament and is willing to prepare for it.
- Appreciates and regularly participates in the liturgy.
- Develops a relationship with Jesus Christ and understands, at some level, the "great commission" (Matthew 28: 16–20).
- Understands what it means to belong to the Catholic community and participate in parish life.
- Views the sacrament of Reconciliation as a privilege rather than a hassle.

Even if you received this sacrament when you were younger, helping someone prepare for Confirmation is a good time to contemplate your answers to these questions:

- Would I be willing and able to receive this sacrament at this juncture of my life?
- What did Confirmation mean to me during my early teens?
- How has being confirmed in the Catholic Church shaped my attitudes, beliefs, and feelings about the Church?

✝

Know someone being confirmed? Sending a little note of blessing and encouragement will make this sacrament even more memorable for them—and also for you. You can also find free electronic greeting cards at www.catholicgreetings.org.

> Preparation *for Confirmation should aim at leading the Christian toward a more intimate union with Christ and a more lively familiarity with the Holy Spirit—his actions, his gifts, and his biddings—in order to be more capable of assuming the apostolic responsibilities of Christian life.*
>
> CCC 1309

Godparents are present at Baptism and sponsors serve a similar function at Confirmation. A godparent may also be a Confirmation sponsor, but this only works if the relationship has panned out as everyone hoped it would. Otherwise, the Confirmation candidate will have to choose a sponsor. The criteria under canon law for godparents and sponsors are the same. So are the other factors, such as choosing someone who is gung ho for Catholicism.

✝

It doesn't matter who is supposed to be preparing for Confirmation. If you're reading this, consider it a sign to study some of what Scripture has to say about the Holy Spirit. Take a look at:

Matthew 3:11, 16; 28:18–20
Luke 11:11–13
John 4:23–24; 7:37–39; 14:25–26; 16:12–15; 20:21–23
Acts 1:3–8; 2:1–41
1 Corinthians 12:4–11
Galatians 5:16–26

You're the Sponsor

Congratulations! You've been blessed with the honor of sponsoring a Confirmation candidate. You've been chosen because you're a spiritually generous person of abiding faith. You also see value in being a member of the Catholic Church.

That's right, you were not chosen for your catechetical knowledge or skills. It's lovely if you have these, but you absolutely do not have to be Mr. or Ms. CCD to be a wonderful sponsor. You are being asked—and called—to be a guide, companion, mentor, and source of encouragement. So while you won't have to memorize dogma, you may want to:

- Enhance your own spiritual fitness through prayer, study, contemplation, and participation in the sacraments.
- Model faith in God, discipleship in Christ, and participation in parish life.
- Share your faith openly and authentically, including struggles with doctrine or dogma.
- Listen carefully and compassionately to the candidate's opinions, beliefs, questions, and concerns.

- Spend quality time with the candidate, which might include volunteering to provide service to the community, attending liturgy, and reviewing Scripture together.
- Stand by the candidate—literally, during the rite and in other ways, like with prayer.

Service to others is not an option for the Christian faithful; it's a requirement. Jesus the Christ calls us to serve one another with compassion, respect, and love. The parish usually provides opportunities for Confirmation candidates to volunteer in the community. If the program isn't structured for entire families to participate together, go ahead and make this happen on your own. Choose a volunteer setting that will enhance your awareness of the Holy Spirit working in your daily life.

How can we not recognize Lazarus, the hungry beggar in the parable (cf. Luke 17:19–31), in the multitude of human beings without bread, a roof or a place to stay? How can we fail to hear Jesus: "As you did it not to one of the least of these, you did it not to me" (Matthew 25:45)?

CCC 2463

Seven Corporal Works of Mercy

Feed the hungry
Give drink to the thirsty
Clothe the naked
Visit the imprisoned
Shelter the homeless
Visit the sick
Bury the dead

Seven Spiritual Works of Mercy

Correct those who need it
Instruct the ignorant
Give counsel to those who need it
Comfort the sorrowful
Suffer wrongs patiently
Forgive all injuries
Pray for the living and the dead

The Holy Eucharist completes Christian initiation. Those who have been raised to the dignity of the royal priesthood by Baptism and configured more deeply to Christ by Confirmation participate with the whole community in the Lord's own sacrifice by means of the Eucharist.

CCC 1322

FIRST EUCHARIST

There's a first time for everything and the first time some-one receives the sacrament of Holy Communion is yet more cause for community celebration. After all, Christ is at the center of our faith. Since Vatican II especially, Catholics in the United States have been more inclined to receive Communion at least once a week. We gather as a community to fulfill Christ's charge to "do this in remem-brance of me" (Luke 22:19). And because coming to the table of the Lord—participating in the Lord's Supper—*is* the Holy Mass, receiving this sacrament is a very big deal indeed.

This blessed event should follow First Reconciliation. Check with your parish to find out when this sacrament is conferred; second grade seems to be the norm these days, al-though adults who enter through the RCIA (Rite of Catholic Initiation for Adults) program first receive this sacrament along with Baptism and Confirmation during Easter Vigil.

All catechesis about First Eucharist will take place in CCD. You are also responsible for teaching your child about this sacrament. And don't expect the CCD teacher to take your tot shopping for an outfit; that glorious task is yours.

PREPARING AT HOME

Check with your parish about how you're expected to participate in First Eucharist preparation. Your child will have CCD
homework that you may be asked to check. If so, you may as
well make this an opportunity to deepen your own ongoing
formation. Some parishes also ask parents to attend preparation classes, if not to reinforce this sacrament's importance,
then to issue instructions about how to escort your little dar-
ling on that special day. What? You're tired of the abundant
rules that seem to surround these sacramental celebrations?
Well, you do have another option. You could choose to make
this a time to reminisce about your own First Eucharist (aka
First Holy Communion). Or you could haul out the baby
book you started at Baptism, contemplating all that has happened since you first consecrated your child to Christ. Finally,
you could indulge your child in the outfit *your* parents
wouldn't let *you* have because "you'll only wear it once and it's
a waste of good money."

✝

Now, about those First Holy Communion outfits. They're
white, of course. By custom, girls get all dolled up in what
look like mini-wedding dresses, complete with tiaras and veils;
boys wear white suits. In reality, the veils have pretty much
given way to flower circlets, and the white suits have been
downsized to white shirts and ties. What you ultimately decide to do will depend on parish guidelines, your family's ethnic heritage, and no shortage of peer pressure. This might be a
good time to teach your child that whining is a venial sin.

And Off to Mass We Go!

Alrighty! Everyone has received the Sacraments of Initiation and everyone is going to Mass—willingly or not.

To some extent, behavior at church is a by-product of what led up to getting there. You can count on bad behavior in church among the juveniles in your family if everyone waits until Sunday morning to pick out an outfit, breakfast is scarfed down at the last possible minute (despite the requirement to fast before receiving the Eucharist), and unmediated battles break out in the car on the way. Heck, you can count on bad *adult* behavior in church under these conditions. Mass should not be a pit stop as you race through Sunday. Recall, if you will, that the dismissal rite includes the injunction to "go in peace," not to huff out as peeved as you were when you arrived.

And yes, daily life impinges. You never planned to cream that deer on the way to Mass, and who knew little Gregory Peter Timothy would get carsick? Setting all that aside, most bad feelings, bad behavior, and bad vibes can be prevented by preparing for Mass as you'd prepare for something illuminating, moving, and joyful. You are, remember, going to be spending time with the Christ. And weren't you excited about this prospect on December 24?

Set out your outfit the night before. Having a break-the-fast snack early enough will make it easier for you to fast an hour before receiving Communion. Say morning prayers before leaving home, and then leave early enough to attend the *entire* Mass. Swooping in for the Creed and beating a hasty retreat after Communion is not only rude and disruptive. It robs you of every opportunity to realize the salutary benefits of church attendance. And if you arrive after the Gospel you've essentialy missed Mass.

Here's another way to enhance your experience: Volunteer to present the gifts (bread and wine) during Mass, perhaps tying this service to a date with special significance for your family.

Preparing for Home-based Communion

Yes, you may receive the Eucharist at home.

This sacrament is available to those who are homebound or too ill to make it to church. And, although home-based Communion may be tied to the Sacrament of Reconciliation or *Viaticum* (aka Last Rights, Extreme Unction), it doesn't have to be.

For this sacred activity, you'll want to prepare sacred space. Press your family altar into service. Or you may transform your dining room table by covering it with a white (or other color, depending on the season) cloth, lighting candles, placing a cross or crucifix nearby, and providing a little vial of holy water. If your housebound loved one is also bedridden, all this can be set up on a night table or dresser top. The priest, deacon, or Eucharistic minister will bring everything else. Once, these ministers would be welcomed at the door with a lighted candle; a lovely custom you might want to revive. And you certainly wouldn't ever have a TV or radio blaring in the background, right?

The Lord Jesus Christ, physician of our souls and bodies . . . has willed that his Church continue, in the power of the Holy Spirit, his work of healing and salvation, even among her own members. This is the purpose of the two sacraments of healing: the sacrament of Penance and the sacrament of Anointing of the Sick.

CCC 1421

*T*he *S*acraments of *H*ealing

RECONCILIATION AND PENANCE

Not all that long ago, "Penance" was called "Confession," a term guaranteed to trigger massive resistance that was dwarfed only by the fear generated by the term "penance." These words basically scared the snot out of wayward believers. The kinder and gentler term, "Reconciliation," reveals the essential nature of this sacrament. Lately, it seems we've gone back to using the word "Penance." No matter what we call it, this sacrament is deep!

This sacrament of healing brings us into deeper communion with the Holy Spirit—Divine Counselor and Comforter. If our goal is to examine actions that separate us from God, and to heal that rift by softening our hearts and changing our behavior, then this name change makes it easier to experience Penance as a gift rather than as a punishment. Additional changes have made this sacrament more . . . uh . . . sacred. These days, you'll probably have to go to the movies to experience the musty privacy of the Confession box (although the sacramental seal of secrecy still holds).

Many contemporary churches offer Communal Penance or Parish Reconciliation services for the parish community. These are generally held during Advent and Lent to help us more fully prepare for Christmas and Easter.

Parish Reconciliation will not, however, exempt you from talking directly with a Confessor (priest). It only means the rite is writ large and hopefully underscores how sin, repentance, and reconciliation may take place in community. You'll listen to Scripture readings, sing a heart-opening hymn or two, and perhaps be led in a guided meditation that serves as an Examination of Conscience. Then it's off to huddle with a priest who may or may not be affiliated with your parish.

When you opt for this sacrament in its individual form, you meet with a priest. Some parishes offer this sacrament in a room with a privacy screen for anyone who might feel creepy about having a face-to-face conversation.

If you're very lucky, you might receive this sacrament from a priest who has enough skill in pastoral counseling to craft an appropriate penance. But even if you're stuck with one who seems to be absolving on automatic ("Say five Hail Marys . . ."), don't let this dissuade you from preparing for this healing sacrament at home.

PREPARING AT HOME

Use prayer and meditation time at home to engage in an Examination of Conscience. But instead of mentally running through a list of possible infractions, do some contemplative writing in preparation for this sacrament. Writing things down will better help you ponder what needs healing. This could be part of an ongoing prayer journal, or a separate notebook in which you write and reflect upon what is and is *not* going on in your life.

These words from the Confiteor provide a useful framework for making an inventory of what needs confessing:

I confess to almighty God,
and to you my brothers and sisters,
that I have sinned through my own fault
in my thoughts and in my words,
in what I have done, and in what I have failed to do. . . .

Need more inspiration? Look up Colossians 3:12–14.

> *Sin is before all else an offense against God, a*
> *rupture of communion with him. At the same*
> *time it damages communion with the Church.*
> *For this reason conversion entails both God's*
> *forgiveness and reconciliation with the Church,*
> *which are expressed and accomplished liturgically*
> *by the sacrament of Penance and Reconciliation.*
>
> CCC 1440

Don't wait for the Church, your pastor, or CCD teachers to convey moral and ethical standards to your children on the eve of First Reconciliation! You'll need to generate awareness and guide children about what constitutes right and wrong long before then. And you'll need to continue home-based education and guidance as your children grow older; teens can get into more trouble than toddlers. The Sacrament of Reconciliation provides a great structure for teaching awareness, self-responsibility, honesty, repentance, and returning to wholeness through faith.

✝

You'll have a much better chance of conveying the value of this sacrament to your kids if you seek it yourself. If you haven't attended Reconciliation in years, plan to do so when your first child participates in First Reconciliation. Now that you're an adult, let yourself see the benefit of relieving guilt, shame, and anxiety by telling the truth, expressing authentic sorrow, and receiving God's forgiveness. Your kids—and adult friends, if you're child-free—will notice when you're fully engaged. Thinking about Reconciliation as the sacrament of healing it's intended to be is one way to ward off your fear of being judged and punished.

Sin

Sin.

Scary word. Right up there with "penance."

Here's another way to understand "sin" and, therefore, why the Sacrament of Reconciliation is a sacrament of healing. Stop thinking that it's about doing "bad" stuff (although the stuff might indeed be bad) and start realizing that it's about doing anything that separates you from God. Whatever separates you from God—God's will, God's love—is a sin. This, by the way, might help you understand the concept of Original Sin. Simply put, God told Adam that he could do anything in Paradise but eat from the tree of the knowledge of good and evil (Genesis 2:16–17). Why? Because such knowledge leads to certain death. Byebye eternal life. Adam and Eve disobeyed and were booted out of the Garden of Eden, separated from God by their disobedience. Their disobedience and subsequent separation is our human legacy and we've been trying to reconnect with God ever since.

Now back to you and what separates *you* from God. Some actions are obvious violations of the Ten Commandments and Christ's teaching about the greatest commandments: " 'Love the Lord your God with all your heart and with all your soul and with all your mind.' This is the first and greatest commandment. And the second is like it: 'Love your neighbor as yourself' " (Matthew 22:37–39). As you prepare for this sacrament of healing, shine the light of consciousness on those times you've deliberately turned away from God and God's love. To what have you turned instead? What have you put between you and God? Take a look at attitudes as well as behaviors and actions. Where have you willfully and knowingly cut yourself off from God? (Hint: *Dreaming* about throttling your boss does not count as a mortal sin, but you might want to examine your wake-time attitudes.)

If you created your own penance, what would it be? What would lead you to a change of heart and behavior? What would bring you deeper into your faith? What would help you realize and appreciate God's infinite mercy and healing love? Would a prayer help you do this? Scripture reading? Serving others to make amends? Asking forgiveness? What? Don't just contemplate these issues before heading off to church, share your insights with your priest or pastor during this time of inquiry and prayer.

> *It is called the sacrament of conversion because it makes sacramentally present Jesus' call to conversion. . . . It is called the sacrament of Penance, since it consecrates the Christian sinner's personal and ecclesial steps of conversion, penance, and satisfaction. It is called the sacrament of confession,*

since the disclosure or confession of sins to a priest
is an essential element of this sacrament. . . . It is
called the sacrament of forgiveness, since by the
priest's sacramental absolution God grants the
penitent "pardon and peace." It is called the sacra-
ment of Reconciliation, because it imparts to the
sinner the life of God who reconciles. . . .

CCC 1423–4

The Formula of Absolution

God, the Father of mercies,
through the death and resurrection of his Son
has reconciled the world to himself
and sent the Holy Spirit among us
for the forgiveness of sins;
through the ministry of the Church
may God give you pardon and peace,
and I absolve you from your sins
in the name of the Father, and of the Son, and of the
Holy Spirit.
Response: Amen.

Rite of Exchange after Absolution

Confessor: Give thanks to the Lord, for God is good.
Penitent: God's mercy endures forever.

Absolution takes away sin, but it does not remedy all the disorders sin has caused. Raised up from sin, the sinner must still recover his full spiritual health by doing something more to make amends for the sin: he must "make satisfaction for" or "expiate" his sins. This satisfaction is also called "penance."

CCC 1459

ANOINTING OF THE SICK

Contrary to popular belief, you do not have to be on the verge of going home to Jesus to receive the Sacrament of Anointing—not these days. If you remember seeing, for real or on TV, a priest hovering over someone's deathbed to administer this sacrament, your memory may be correct, but dated. These are no longer the Last Rites but part of an ongoing understanding that prayer and faith are integral to healing, if not curing, sickness.

Anointing the sick one's forehead and hands with blessed oil for this sacrament extends the healing embrace of Christ. The Sacrament of Anointing can be celebrated at any point, as the illness runs its course. It can be received more than once. Double dipping is allowed! Optimally, this sacrament is celebrated within the context of a parish gathering. But if illness prevents church attendance, it can also be celebrated at home, in a hospital, or in a rehabilitation facility, with or without family gathered.

As for which illnesses are eligible, the Church recognizes that sickness can strike body, mind, and spirit. Anxiety disorders, addictions, or unhealthy relationships are as worthy of anointing as, say, something terminal. While you do not need a note from your primary care physician to receive this sacrament, you *will* need a priest.

The first grace of this sacrament [Anointing of the Sick] is one of strengthening, peace, and courage to overcome the difficulties that go with the condition of serious illness or the frailty of old age. This grace is a gift of the Holy Spirit, who renews trust and faith in God.

CCC 1520

PREPARING AT HOME

Long before you call the church for a pastoral sick call, gather family and friends together for prayer support. There's ample evidence to suggest that intercessory prayer does work wonders. To that end, you can prepare for the Sacrament of Anointing by hosting group prayer in your home that might include, but not be limited to, praying the Rosary (see Appendix B). And if you're the caregiver, do request prayer for yourself. This role can be as physically exhausting and emotionally debilitating as whatever illness your loved one suffers.

✝

When serious and possibly terminal illness is involved, contact your parish office to find out how to receive:

- Home-based sick calls by a priest.
- Home-based Communion by an Extraordinary Minister of Holy Communion.
- Parish support for meals and transportation.

And no, you do not have to pay for these services. If, at some point, you'd like to make a financial donation to your church, no one will stop you! Mass cards, with a stipend of as little as five dollars, are an exception. A Mass card lets the recipient know that the gift of prayer, in the form of a Mass, is being said for someone. And while most people get Mass cards when someone dies, a Mass can also be dedicated to someone still among the living.

Prayer of Anointing

Through this holy anointing,
may the Lord in his love and mercy
help you with the grace of the Holy Spirit.
May the Lord who frees you from sin
save you and raise you up. Amen.

When you make a sick call you can make your visit a blessing by:

- Calling in advance to check on visiting times. Once there, you'll get a better sense of how you may be helpful (e.g., doing a load of laundry, dropping letters off at the post office).

- Using good judgment about what to bring. Do not bring flowers to someone who is hooked up to an oxygen tank, candy to someone with diabetes complications, or magazines to anyone who has just had eye surgery. If the illness has been going on for a while or you know there have been lots of visitors, showing up with a pound of coffee, packages of hot/cold cups, or boxes of tissues will mean more than you can imagine.

- Pay attention to the time and don't overstay your welcome. In some instances, fifteen minutes is more than enough. Under other circumstances, you may be inclined to stay longer, sitting silently and prayerfully with the sick person or caregiver.

Note: These suggestions also apply for funeral vigils and wakes.

Just as the sacraments of Baptism, Confirmation, and the Eucharist form a unity called "the sacraments of Christian initiation," so too it can be said that Penance, the Anointing of the Sick and the Eucharist as viaticum constitute at the end of Christian life "the sacraments that prepare for our heavenly homeland or the sacraments that complete the earthly pilgrimage."

CCC 1525

So, What Did *Happen to the Last Rites?*

You *liked* the drama and mystery of deathbed scenes you saw at the movies. And while you aren't planning to commit any mortal sins that'll need confessing, you were imagining something poignant during your last minutes of embodiment. Well, you may indeed have this; it's *Viaticum* (communion for the dying), which includes the Sacrament of Reconciliation and the Eucharist. This may take place at home, and is powerfully moving when family members participate in receiving the Eucharist.

At some point, it *is* time to say final good-byes, but only here on Earth. For Catholic believers, death isn't really the end. It's the beginning of eternal life. The customs and traditions of All Souls' Day reinforce this belief, as do prayers at Mass for the living and the dead. So it should come as no surprise that grief and joy vie for emotional space at church (where a funeral Mass may be *celebrated*) and at your home or the funeral home (where the "visitation" or "wake" and Vigil are usually held). Both the wake and the funeral liturgy are intended to provide comfort and support for the bereaved. Exactly how that support manifests will depend in part on the family's ethnic tradition. Customs include:

- Kneeling and praying before the open casket.
- Praying the Rosary with the family, other bereaved, and guests.
- Whooping it up with food, drink, and stories about the dear departed after the funeral.

- Making a charitable donation instead of sending flowers.
- Sending flowers or live plants to the home well *after* the funeral.
- Sending a Mass card.
- Preparing meals and snacks for the family and their out-of-town funeral guests.
- Providing housing and transportation, if needed, for out-of-town funeral guests.
- Arranging childcare so that the living can grieve in peace.
- Praying a novena (nine nights of prayer) that starts the night of the funeral and ends with a feast to honor the deceased.

Prayer for the Faithful Departed

Eternal rest grant unto them, O Lord.
Response: And let perpetual light shine upon them. May their souls and the souls of all the faithful departed, through the mercy of God, rest in peace. Amen.

Two other sacraments, Holy Orders and Matrimony, are directed toward the salvation of others; if they contribute as well to personal salvation, it is through service to others that they do so. They confer a particular mission in the Church and serve to build up the People of God.

CCC 1534

Sacraments of Vocation and Service

MARRIAGE (HOLY MATRIMONY)

The Church didn't get around to making marriage an official sacrament, and thus a special grace, until the Fourth Lateran Council in 1215. It kept a grip, one that got increasingly tighter, on the institution until marriages were placed under civil law by France's Napoleonic Code during the eighteenth century. Still, since this is a sacrament, there's no shortage of preparation required for a regulation Catholic wedding.

Today, if you want a church wedding that includes a Nuptial Mass, you'll need a priest and two witnesses. Actually, if you want a Nuptial Mass, it has to take place in a church—forget about that outdoor wedding. If you insist on making everyone crazy by holding something outdoors, you cannot have a Mass but a deacon may preside over the ceremony.

Like all the other sacraments, the Sacrament of Marriage is also celebrated in the context of community. The entire community joins in celebrating and witnessing the commitment of two people to one another and to God. Technically, any parishioner may attend a Nuptial Mass and, if attending, should fully participate in the liturgy. Just don't plan on going to the wedding reception without an invitation. And don't plan on leaping off the pew to voice last-minute objections. You'll have had your chance to challenge anyone's marital fitness when the wedding banns are publicly posted on three consecutive Sundays before the ceremony.

The Church makes a valiant effort to shape up the starry-eyed for marital realities as a sacrament (and a *lot* of secular work). Even before divorce rates among Catholics started matching those of the general population, the Church required a series of pre-wedding inquiries for engaged couples. While these happen at church, much of the preparation can take place at home.

Preparation for marriage can—and probably should—take quite a while, and not so there's time to pick out table linens that match the flowers that match the hors d'oeuvres. Lengthy preparation is required because this is a sacrament of vocation as profound as the Sacrament of Holy Orders. Marriage joins two people into a holy union that, with or without children, is the foundation on which the domestic Church is built. For after all, "where two or more are gathered in my name, I will be there with them" (Matthew 18:20).

> *The sacrament of Matrimony signifies the union of Christ and the Church. It gives spouses the grace to love each other with the love with which Christ has loved his Church; the grace of the sacrament thus perfects the human love of spouses. . . .*
>
> CCC 1661

Preparing at Home

Most parishes require a pre-wedding conversation at least nine months before the ceremony and definitely before a single invitation is engraved. A conversation (i.e., interview) with a priest or deacon is the first step and is designed to both elicit and provide information. It should be friendly, warm, and inviting. Some parishes may require engaged couples to complete a diocesan questionnaire about values, attitudes, and beliefs. Be prepared to discuss:

- What you love about each other.
- Why you're getting married at this juncture.
- What you expect from marriage.
- Your Catholic upbringing and education.
- Why you want to be married in the Catholic Church.
- Your intentions about having children and raising them in the Faith.
- Anything that might be in the way of having a Catholic wedding with a Nuptial Mass.

And be prepared to receive information about:

- Marriage as a sacrament.
- What constitutes marital fitness and a "free union."
- Dealing with special situations (e.g., when one or both parties have been divorced, interfaith marriages, blended families).
- Reserving a wedding date that accounts for liturgical calendar restrictions.

- Attending Pre-Cana or marriage preparation classes or retreats.

Rest assured that details of choosing music within Church guidelines, having hysterics about flowers and where to have the reception will be discussed later with parish staff and your mother.

✝

Prepare for the Sacrament of Marriage by examining your individual fitness, compatibility as a couple, and ability to communicate about family life, health, money, work, politics, sex, family planning, children, faith, and religious observance. Preparation should include coming to grips with past or present trauma, addiction, and emotional health issues. To this end, in addition to Pre-Cana sessions, consider going for premarital counseling with a social worker or psychologist specifically trained to work with couples. This is especially important if any topic covered during the Pre-Cana or marriage preparation program raises questions, triggers reactions, causes distress, or generates conflict.

✝

By God's grace, you and your spouse will be married for a very long time, so it's time to build a strong spiritual foundation for your lives together. As your prepare for the Sacrament of Marriage, get into the habit of:

- Praying with and for each other.
- Serving each other with gladness and thanksgiving.
- Blessing each other with the sign of the cross.

- Showing each other honor and respect in private *and* in public.
- Modeling marriage as a vocation.

Collect documents! In addition to the civil license, which usually requires a three-day waiting period, you need to provide copies of Baptism, First Eucharist, and Confirmation certificates, certificates of completion for any required Pre-Cana programs, evidence of annulment if previously married, possibly letters of a "free state" verifying that the marriage may happen within the Church, and possibly documentation attesting to the ability of your chosen witnesses to play that role.

What Are Those Feelings? Jitters?

You've wanted a church wedding ever since you trotted down the aisle for First Eucharist in your frilly frock or smart little white suit. Now you're not even one quarter of the way through the pre-wedding process and you want to bag the church, deck the priest, throttle the music director, and run off to—anywhere.

Don't.

Instead, make a solemn vow with your beloved to tough out what you think are distressing, irritating, or convoluted requirements. Bravely consider that your negative reaction to anything the Church requires may in fact be a warning sign. If you can't hack the hassles of *getting* married, it's doubtful that you'll suddenly be able to hack the hassles of *being* married—with or without children.

Impediments to having the church wedding of your dreams are a signal to *s l o w   d o w n*, not speed up the process. If you're sorely tempted to elope, remember the radically social nature of the sacraments. Come back to the Church, the Body of Christ has arms to embrace you.

HOLY ORDERS

Long gone are the days when every Catholic family could count on at least one son entering the priesthood, but that doesn't mean it couldn't happen again!

Currently the vocations of priest and deacon are open only to Catholic men, based on the Church's distinction of emerging from Jesus Christ (a man)—one, long unbroken line that started with the twelve apostles (men). And despite the fact that some of the twelve apostles were married, Catholic priests must be single. The Eastern Orthodox Church allows its priests and deacons to marry, but we have a slew of medieval property rights disputes to thank for this requirement in the West. The whole business is too convoluted and beside the point to delve into here, although in the Strange-but-True Department, there have been cases where a married cleric from another Christian denomination has converted to Catholicism *and* remained a priest. Permanent deacons (men) may be married.

God only knows what the future holds for those who feel called to receive the Sacrament of Holy Orders. What we know is that this is not a career path open to just any man. This is work that someone is called by God to pursue. So if receiving the Sacrament of Holy Orders is the result of a "calling" or vocation, can there be much preparation at home? Certainly!

For some, preparation may start in childhood, for others, much later. In any event, the process of discernment involves prayer, conversation, prayer, self-examination, prayer, research into different orders, prayer, participation, prayer, counsel from others, and prayer. It also helps to enthusiastically encourage anyone interested in becoming a priest or deacon. After all, this is a sacrament of vocation and service, both to faith and to the community of the faithful.

No one has the right *to receive the sacrament of Holy Orders. Indeed no one claims this office for himself; he is called to it by God. Anyone who thinks he recognizes the signs of God's call to the ordained ministry must humbly submit his desire to the authority of the Church, who has the responsibility and right to call someone to receive orders. Like every grace this sacrament can be* received *only as an unmerited gift.*

CCC 1578

You're Invited to an Ordination

You know what's an appropriate gift for someone celebrating any of the other sacraments, but you've been invited to an ordination and you're stumped. Well, not if you think it through.

Remember, this is someone who probably has just gotten out of seminary and is committed to a life of material simplicity. The newly ordained priest neither needs nor wants yet another Bible, set of rosary beads, crucifix, holy water font, scapular, Miraculous Medal, portable *prie-dieu*, *Viaticum* kit, or life-sized statue of the Blessed Virgin Mother.

Think graduate student. Think newlywed. That should safely guide you to bestow housewares, electronic equipment, appliances, and clothing—or gift certificates for these items. Cash!

As for the new permanent deacon—if he's married—give his wife a gift for surviving his education and training. Of course, you can never go wrong making a charitable contribution to a social justice ministry or another worthy cause.

AFTERWORD

AT THE START of this project, I sent frantic, 3 A.M. emails to my editor and agent. "Get someone else to write this," I begged, "I'm not worthy." They laughed at me. So I started whining to friends, who laughed at me some more and, being friends, also groaned. "Have you looked around your home lately?" one finally asked.

Ah yes, my home.

I've taken to referring to it with great affection as "The Hermitage." A few years ago, I drastically downsized (again) for any number of reasons, mostly having to do with going inward—in an outgoing kind of way. These days, it's just the cats and me; Julian of Norwich goes suburban. "And lots of Jesus," one friend always adds with a good-natured yip whenever I muse out loud about such things.

She probably means that you'll find icons and other images of Jesus, the *Theotokos*, and archangels throughout my home. In my office, for example, is a framed "Consecration of the Family to the Sacred Heart" certificate done in that wonderfully goopy airbrushed style of bad liturgical art. I found this treasure over a decade ago in a junk shop that had priced it at ten dollars. I was taking my first soul sabbatical at the time, had no steady income, and when I had any cash, rarely walked around with more than a dollar in my wallet—as a spiritual practice.

For weeks, I daydreamed about having that picture. Two months later, I went back to the shop with the ten dollars I'd finally scraped up. Jesus was marked down to eight bucks, which I took as a powerful sign; my Lord would be mine. Of course I bought it, and have kept Him in my office ever since. The image may drive lapsed Catholics a little nuts, but I don't care. It gives me a feeling of comfort and safety to look past the thorns into the heart of Jesus. Sometimes, when I shift my vision to take in the sight of his wounded hands as they hold open his robe, the enormity of the Crucifixion sweeps through my consciousness and I actually understand what a huge, big deal God's love is for minutes at a time.

My attempt at the Vladimir Mother of God, under the tutelage of iconographer Peter Pearson, is in my living room. An earlier effort to paint—although he would say "write"—an icon of Archangel Gabriel, under the tutelage of iconographer Vladislav Andrejev, monitors the phone in my kitchen. Both icons once played a powerful role in diffusing the considerable crankiness of the Macedonian immigrant who grumbled his way through a washer-dryer installation last year. "We icons Orthodox have," he said with great delight once he emerged from the basement and saw these familiar images. "Catholic," I replied, pointing to myself. (The icons provided a way to talk about prayer with the two apple-cheeked Mormon boys I welcomed in for a chat that lasted two hours.)

I have crosses on the walls. If music is playing, it's usually either chant or a Latin Mass setting. Years ago, I switched from *Nag Champa* to frankincense. The latest issue of the *Magnificat* follows me from room to room, along with the cats. Guess who stands watch over *my* garden? A reproduction of Robert Lentz's icon of St. Edith Stein of Auschwitz provides strange comfort from my desk-side bulletin board. I finally stopped whipping the rosary beads and the little purple glow-in-the-dark cross off my nightstand before my mother's visits.

"So, have you converted?" she asks every time she calls. I resist the mighty temptation to respond with "Duh," like a surly teenager. I look back over the years of being a Jew-turned-Christian practicing Catholic and realize how long it has taken me to simply say, "Yes." It's both simple and enormously complex—just like the business of creating a Catholic home.

If you visit The Hermitage for tea, I'm sure you'll notice all the stuff and the books, but I don't think that's what makes it feel like a Catholic Christian home. Instead, I hope it feels that way because of things that are larger but less obvious. I hope it feels like a Catholic Christian home because I've come to order my interior and exterior life according to the liturgical calendar; because even if I don't pray the Daily Office, I always mean to; because I know the proper response to just about everything is "Thanks and glory be to God." This is what I hope. And, this is what I pray.

—THE THIRD WEEK OF LENT, 2003

"May the Lord bless you
and keep you;
May the Lord make his face to shine
upon you
and be gracious unto you;
May the Lord turn his face
toward you
and give you peace."

NUMBERS 6:24–26

APPENDIX A

*M*ARKING *T*IME

*Y*OU KNOW THE CALENDAR stuck to your refrigerator with fruit magnets? Setting aside Genesis 1:14–19, ever wonder how days, months, and years came into being? The subject, albeit fascinating, is much too convoluted to present in detail. Still, because the liturgical calendar includes "moveable feasts," here's a brief overview.

Today's universally used calendar is based on the Earth's movement around the sun. Each year (of either 365 or 366 days) is divided into twelve months. Dividing the year into days and months this way has been around for centuries, as have mathematical formulae for calculating leap years.

Until the sixteenth century, everyone used the solar calendar Julius Caesar concocted in 45 B.C., his attempt to organize chaos. The "Julian" calendar lost its primacy after the "Gregorian" solar calendar was constructed by Pope Gregory XIII in 1582.

It should only be this straightforward.

But it isn't, thanks to a corresponding history of disputes about how to accurately determine the length of the tropical year. Now add to that monkish attempts during the sixth and eighth centuries to establish rules for counting years. And yet these mind-numbing calculations are simple when compared to those used to locate moveable feasts and fasts.

KNOWING YOUR A, B, C, D, AND E'S

Here's what the alphabet soup with historical dates means:

B.C. . . . . Before Christ

A.D.   In the Year of the Lord

                                       (*Anno Domini*)

B.C.E. Before the Common Era

C.E. . . . . Common Era

Which ones to use? Because the abbreviations B.C. and A.D. assert the primacy and centrality of Jesus Christ, texts that involve other faith traditions generally use B.C.E. and C.E. notations.

✝

Surely you've noticed how Lent sometimes seems to arrive "early," or that Ordinary Time occasionally seems extremely "long." This is because Easter hippity-hops around the spring months relative to the full moon, the fullness of which is also a source of dispute. Is it the "real" (astronomical) full moon or the "official" (relative to the vernal equinox)? This requires knowing the Golden Number and another mathematical measurement, the Epact, both of which you'll be spared reading about here.

Next, factor in the connection between Easter and the Jewish celebration of Passover. If there's agreement about anything, it's that the Last Supper was a Passover Seder. So, you might rightfully expect to celebrate the death and resurrection of Jesus the Christ *after* Passover. Great expectation, but unlike the pagan-derived Roman solar calendar, the Jewish calendar is based on the sun *and* the moon. As a result, the first night of Passover may not necessarily line up perfectly with Holy Thursday. In any event, the Nicene Council of A.D. 325 formally substituted Easter for Passover. (The Council also moved Sabbath from Friday at sundown to dawn on Sunday.)

So when is Easter Sunday? That's the question, right?

Easter Sunday is celebrated on the first Sunday *after* the first "official" full moon *after* the "official" vernal (spring) equinox on March 21. This date determines when Lent begins, and when Ascension and Pentecost are celebrated. The ensuing ripple effect is intensified by celebrating the feast of Christ the King the Sunday on or after November 20, then placing the first Sunday in Advent relative to that. This is why so-called Ordinary Time after Pentecost and later, Epiphany, may end up feeling compressed.

Meanwhile, just because we believe in "one, holy, catholic, and apostolic Church," doesn't mean we're all on the same calendar page.

Our Orthodox cousins, for example, still use the Julian calendar to calculate Easter. Many, but not all, Orthodox churches celebrate Christmas on January 7 instead of on December 25. The Orthodox ecclesiastical year begins on September 8 with the Nativity of the Mother of God. Few of the clergy, confessors, martyrs, prophets, and virgins venerated by the Orthodox Church also show up on the Latin Rite calendar. Who rates an appearance on both calendars has to do with the Great Schism between Constantinople and Rome in A.D. 1054. Generally speaking, Orthodox churches don't recognize the canonization of anyone after that parting of the ways.

*𝒯*HE *ℛ*OSARY

*ℒ*IKE MANY OTHER uniquely Catholic devotions, the Rosary has its adherents and critics. Nevertheless, this is an enduring prayer practice, existing long before the Dominican Rosary gained universal acceptance.

As early as the fifth century, when psalms were routinely memorized, 150 beads were used to keep track of them. By the eleventh century, beads were used to pray the 150 Our Fathers (the Poor Man's Psalter) and to contemplate the life of Christ. At some point the Angelic Salutation ("Hail Mary, full of grace. The Lord is with you. Blessed are you among women, and blessed is the fruit of your womb, Jesus.") was added. By the twelfth century, 150 Our Fathers were replaced by (shorter) Hail Marys, possibly because the laity simply didn't have the same amount of time available as did monastics for prayer.

Despite this venerable history, St. Dominic de Guzmán receives almost total credit for inventing the Rosary during the thirteenth century. Legend has it that the now familiar form—150 beads separated into five groupings of ten Hail Mary beads separated by an Our Father bead—was delivered via vision to him by the Blessed Virgin Mother herself.

From the sixteenth century until the twenty-first century, the Rosary was recited in three sets of five mysteries (i.e., the Joyful, Sorrowful, and Glorious). At the beginning of the twenty-first century, Pope John Paul II suggested another set of mysteries (i.e., the Mysteries of Light, or Luminous Mysteries).

Rosary devotion was florid during the fifteenth and sixteenth centuries, despite efforts to eradicate the practice by such formidable opponents as Queen Elizabeth I in her role as head of the Church of England. By the seventeenth century, Marian veneration had exceeded the *dulia* (honor) properly accorded to saints and the *hyperdulia* rightfully due Mary, Holy Mother of God.

Although displaced devotion would periodically come under critical scrutiny, praying the Rosary has never disappeared. Neither has Mary. Apparitions of Mary—real or imagined—would inspire spates of even more adoration throughout the centuries. By the time Vatican Council II convened in 1962, Mariolatry had emerged again. Among other things, reports of parishioners (perhaps *your* grandmother?) praying the Rosary during Mass led to Pope Paul VI issuing "Guidelines for Devotion to the Blessed Virgin" in 1974. These guidelines remind the fervid faithful how the Rosary is supposed to gently draw us into meditating on the mysteries of the life, death, and resurrection of Christ. It's not meant to be a method for racking up repetitions or the wordy babbling that Jesus cautioned against (Matthew 6:7).

Praying the Rosary with others enhances the experience of being in the Body of Christ. During the tenth century, many Catholic families would gather together daily to pray the Rosary and the Divine Office, a ritual that would survive into the twentieth century. Alas, the family Rosary was sometimes treated like a forced march to heaven. You probably know people raised with this tradition who have nothing good to say about it! Even more reason to restore this practice to its power and beauty.

An Extremely Concise Guide to Praying the Rosary

It's easy to find pamphlets, wallet cards, and entire books about praying the Rosary. Rummage through your files and you'll probably find the one you were given during CCD or RCIA. Until then, perhaps this will refresh your memory.

1. Begin on the Crucifix by making the Sign of the Cross and saying, "In the name of the Father and of the Son and of the Holy Spirit. Amen"
2. Recite the Apostles' Creed
3. Pray the Our Father on the first large bead
4. Pray the Hail Mary on the next three small beads
5. Pray the Glory Be on the next large bead, announce the first Mystery, then pray the Our Father
6. Meditate on the first Mystery while praying the Hail Mary on the next ten beads (a decade)
7. On the next large bead, pray the Glory Be, announce the second Mystery, then pray the Our Father
8. Meditate on the second Mystery while praying the Hail Mary on the next decade
9. Continue until you've meditated on all five events that comprise either the Joyful, Sorrowful, Glorious, or Luminous Mysteries
10. End by praying Hail, Holy Queen

> *The Church rightly honors "the Blessed Virgin with special devotion. From the most ancient times the Blessed Virgin has been honored with the title of 'Mother of God,' to whose protection the faithful fly in all their dangers and needs . . . This very special devotion . . . differs essentially from the adoration which is given to the incarnate Word and equally to the Father and the Holy Spirit, and greatly fosters this adoration."*
>
> CCC 971

Hail Mary

Hail Mary, full of grace. The Lord is with thee. Blessed art thou among women, and blessed is the fruit of thy womb, Jesus.

Holy Mary, Mother of God, pray for us sinners, now and at the hour of our death. Amen.

Glory to the Father

Glory to the Father, and to the Son, and to the Holy Spirit. As it was in the beginning, is now, and will be forever. Amen.

Hail, Holy Queen

Hail, holy queen, mother of mercy, our life, our sweetness, and our hope.

To you we cry, poor banished children of Eve; to you we send up our sighs, mourning and weeping in this

valley of tears. Turn then, O most gracious advocate, your eyes of mercy toward us, and after this our exile, show unto us the blessed fruit of your womb, Jesus. O clement, O loving, O sweet virgin Mary.
Pray for us, O holy Mother of God.

Response: That we may be made worthy of the promises of Christ, let us pray; O God, whose only begotten Son, by his life, death, and Resurrection, has purchased for us the rewards of eternal life, grant, we beseech you, that meditating upon these mysteries of the most holy Rosary of the Blessed Virgin Mary, we may imitate what they contain and obtain what they promise. Through the same Christ our Lord. Amen.

MYSTERIES OF THE ROSARY

The Joyful Mysteries

Meditated on Mondays, Thursdays, Sundays during Advent, and Sundays from Epiphany until Lent

1. The Annunciation.
2. The Visitation.
3. The Nativity.
4. The Presentation.
5. Finding Jesus in the Temple.

The Sorrowful Mysteries

Meditated on Tuesdays, Fridays, and daily from Ash Wednesday until Easter Sunday

1. Agony in the Garden.
2. Scourging at the Pillar.
3. Crowning with Thorns.
4. Carrying the Cross.
5. The Crucifixion.

The Glorious Mysteries

Meditated on Wednesdays and Saturdays from Easter until Advent

1. The Resurrection.
2. The Ascension.
3. The Descent of the Holy Spirit.
4. The Assumption of Mary.
5. The Crowning of Mary.

The Mysteries of Light (Luminous Mysteries)

Meditated on Sundays

1. Christ's Baptism in the Jordan River.
2. Christ's self-revelation at the marriage at Cana.
3. Christ announces the kingdom of God and invites conversion.
4. The Transfiguration.
5. The institution of the Eucharist at the Last Supper.

APPENDIX C

$\mathcal{M}$ARY

$\mathcal{A}$M I THE ONLY ONE who wants to have in one handy location all the titles ascribed to Mary? I think not, and so I've compiled a fairly comprehensive but not exhaustive list of the ways Catholics refer to Mary. (Her Hebrew name appears in texts as either Maryam or Miriam, depending on the translation.)

This is quite the compendium, one that provides an almost daily name upon which to meditate. Indeed, you might consider doing just that to deepen your understanding of, appreciation for, and devotion to Mary. Which titles immediately capture your imagination? Which ones provide familiar comfort? Which ones seem quirky or downright weird? Personally speaking, I'm hard pressed to choose between "Neck of the Mystical Body" and "Undug Well of Remission's Waters," although "Paradise Fenced Against the Serpent" is a strong contender.

Notice how your favorite aspect of Mary shifts according to your life circumstances and spiritual condition. Note also how alphabetizing this roster makes for some very interesting juxtapositions!

Adam's Deliverance
Advocate of Eve
Advocate of Sinners
All Chaste
All Fair and Immaculate
All Good
Aqueduct of Grace
Ark Gilded by the Holy Spirit
Ark of the Covenant
Blessed Among Women
Blessed Virgin Mary
Bridal Chamber of the Lord
Bride of Christ
Bride of Heaven
Bride of the Canticle
Bride of the Father
Cause of Our Joy
Chosen Before the Ages
Comfort of Christians
Comforter of the Afflicted
Consoler of the Afflicted
Co-Redemptrix
Court of the Eternal King
Created Temple of the Creator
Crown of Virginity
Daughter of Men
David's Daughter
Deliverer From All Wrath
Deliverer of Christian Nations
Destroyer of Heresies
Dispenser of Grace
Dwelling Place for God
Dwelling Place of the Spirit
Earth Unsown
Earth Untouched and Virginal
Eastern Gate

Ever Green and Fruitful
Ever Virgin
Exalted Above the Angels
Fleece of Heavenly Rain
Flower of Carmel
Flower of Jesse's Root
Formed Without Sin
Forthbringer of God
Forthbringer of the Ancient of
    Days
Forthbringer of the Tree of Life
Fountain of Living Water
Fountain Sealed
Free from Every Stain
Full of Grace
Garden Enclosed
Gate of Heaven
God's Eden
God's Olive Tree
God's Vessel
Handmaid of the Lord
Healing Balm of Integrity
Health of the Sick
Helper of All in Danger
Help of Christians
Holy in Soul and Body
Hope of Christians
House Built by Wisdom
House of Gold
Immaculate
Immaculate Conception
Immaculate Heart
Immaculate Mother
Immaculate Queen
Immaculate Virgin
Incorruptible Wood of the Ark

Inventrix of Grace

Inviolate

Joseph's Spouse

Kingly Throne

King's Mother

Lady Most Venerable

Lady of Charity

Lady of Counsel

Lady of the Golden Heart

Lady of Good Help

Lady of the Holy Souls

Lady of Mercy

Lady of Peace

Lady of Perpetual Help

Lady of Prompt Succor

Lady of Providence

Lady of Ransom

Lady of the Rosary

Lady of Sorrows

Lady of Tears

Lady of Victory

Lamp Unquenchable

Life-Giver to Posterity

Light Cloud of Heavenly Rain

Lily Among Thorns

Living Temple of the Deity

Loom of the Incarnation

Mediatrix

Mediatrix and Conciliatrix

Mediatrix of All Grace

Mediatrix of Salvation

Mediatrix of the Mediator

Minister of Life

Mirror of Justice

More Beautiful than Beauty

More Glorious than Paradise

More Gracious than Grace

More Holy than the Cherubim, the Seraphim, and the Entire Angelic Hosts

Morning Star

Most Venerable

Mother Most Admirable

Mother Most Amiable

Mother Most Pure

Mother of Christians

Mother of Christ's Members

Mother of Divine Grace

Mother of God

Mother of Good Counsel

Mother of Jesus Christ

Mother of Men

Mother of Our Creator

Mother of Our Head

Mother of Our Savior

Mother of the Church

Mother of the Mystical Body

Mother of Wisdom

Mother Undefiled

My Body's Healing

My Soul's Saving

Mystical Rose

Nature's Re-Creation

Nature's Restoration

Neck of the Mystical Body

Never Fading Wood

New Eve

Nourisher of God and Man

Olive Tree of the Father's Compassion

Only Bridge of God to Men

Paradise Fenced Against the
  Serpent
Paradise of Innocence and
  Immortality
Paradise of the Second Adam
Paradise Planted by God
Patroness and Protectoress
Perfume of Faith
Preserved from All Sin
Protectoress from All Hurt
Star of the Sea
Queen of All Saints
Queen of Angels
Queen of the Apostles
Queen of Creation
Queen of Heaven
Queen of Heaven and Earth
Queen of Martyrs
Queen of Peace
Queen Unconquered
Refuge in Time and Danger
Refuge of Sinners
Reparatrix
Reparatrix of Her Parents
Reparatrix of the Lord World
Rich in Mercy
Rose Ever Blooming
Sanctuary of the Holy Spirit
Scepter of Orthodoxy
Seat of Wisdom
Second Eve
Singular Vessel of Devotion
Sister and Mother
Spiritual Vessel
Spotless Dove of Beauty
Star of the Sea

Suppliant for Sinners
Surpassing Eden's Gardens
Surpassing the Heavens
Surpassing the Seraphim
Sweet Flowering and Gracious
  Mercy
Tabernacle of God
Tabernacle of the Word
Temple Divine
Temple Indestructible
Temple of the Lord's Body
Theotokos
Throne of the King
Tower of David
Tower of Ivory
Tower Unassailable
Treasure House of Life
Treasure of Immortality
Treasure of the World
  Undefiled
Undefiled Treasure of
  Virginity
Undug Well of Remission's
  Waters
Unlearned in the Ways of Eve
Unplowed Field of Heaven's
  Bread
Unwatered Vineyard of
  Immortality's Wine
Vessel of Honor
Victor Over the Serpent
Virgin Most Faithful
Virgin Most Merciful
Virgin Most Powerful
Virgin Most Prudent
Virgin Most Pure

Virgin Mother
Virgin of Virgins
Wedded to God
Woman Clothed with the Sun
Workshop of the Incarnation

ESSENTIAL PRAYERS

The Apostles' Creed

I believe in God, the Father almighty,
   creator of heaven and earth.
   And in Jesus Christ, his only Son, our Lord;
   who was conceived by the power of the Holy Spirit
      and born of the Virgin Mary.
   He suffered under Pontius Pilate,
      was crucified, died, and was buried.
   He descended into hell;
   on the third day he rose again from the dead;
   he ascended into heaven,
      and is seated at the right hand of the Father.
   He will come again to judge the living and the dead.
I believe in the Holy Spirit,
         the holy catholic Church,
         the communion of saints,
         the forgiveness of sins,
         the resurrection of the body,
         and life everlasting. Amen.

... *the Creed's final "Amen" repeats and con-
firms its first words: "I believe." To believe is to
say "Amen" to God's words, promises and commandments; to entrust oneself completely to him
who is the "Amen" of infinite love and perfect
faithfulness. The Christian's everyday life will
then be the "Amen" to the "I believe" of our baptismal profession of faith.*

CCC 1064

Profession of Faith

We believe in one God,
the Father, the Almighty,
maker of heaven and earth,
of all that is seen and unseen.
We believe in one Lord, Jesus Christ,
the only son of God,
eternally begotten of the Father,
God from God, Light from Light,
true God from true God,
begotten, not made, one in Being with the Father.
Through him all things were made.
For us and for our salvation
he came down from heaven
by the power of the Holy Spirit
he was born of the Virgin Mary, and became
man.
For our sake he was crucified under Pontius Pilate;
he suffered, died, and was buried.

On the third day he rose again
  in fulfillment of the Scriptures;
he ascended into heaven
  and is seated at the right hand of the Father.
He will come again in glory to judge the living and the dead,
  and his kingdom will have no end.
We believe in the Holy Spirit, the Lord, the giver of life,
  who proceeds from the Father and the Son.
  With the Father and the Son he is worshiped and glorified.
  He has spoken through the Prophets.
  We believe in one holy, catholic, and apostolic Church.
  We acknowledge one baptism for the forgiveness of sins.
  We look for the resurrection of the dead,
    and the life of the world to come. Amen.

The Lord's Prayer

Our Father,
who art in heaven,
hallowed be thy name;
thy kingdom come;
thy will be done on earth as it is in heaven.
Give us this day our daily bread;
and forgive us our trespasses
as we forgive those who trespass against us;
and lead us not into temptation,
but deliver us from evil. Amen.

Simple and faithful trust, humble and joyous assurance are the proper dispositions for one who prays the Our Father.

CCC 2797

Prayers to the Holy Spirit

Come, Holy Spirit, fill the hearts of your faithful,
And kindle in them the fire of your love.
Send forth your Spirit and they shall be created.
And you shall renew the face of the earth.
Lord, by the light of the Holy Spirit
You have taught the hearts of your faithful.
In the same Spirit
Help us relish what is right
and always rejoice in your consolation.
We ask this through Christ our Lord. Amen.

O, Holy Spirit, beloved of my soul . . .
    I adore You.

Enlighten me, guide me, strengthen me, console me.

Tell me what I should do . . .
    give me Your orders.

I promise to submit myself
to all that You desire of me
and to accept all that You
permit to happen to me.

Let me only know Your will. Amen.

Doxology (Trinity Prayer/Prayer of Praise)

Glory be to the Father, and to the Son, and to the Holy
Spirit.
As it was in the beginning, is now and ever shall be,
world without end. Amen.

The Jesus Prayer

Lord Jesus Christ,
Son of God,
have mercy on me, a sinner. Amen.

Penitential Rite/Confiteor

I confess to you almighty God,
and to you my brothers and sisters,
that I have sinned through my own fault
in my thoughts and in my words,
in what I have done, and in what I have failed to do;
and I ask blessed Mary, ever virgin,
all the angels and saints,
and you, my brothers and sisters,
to pray for me to the Lord our God.
May almighty God have mercy on us, forgive us our
sins, and bring us to life everlasting. Amen.

Act of Contrition

My God, I am sorry for my sins.
In choosing to do wrong and failing to do good,
I have sinned against you,
whom I should love above all things.
I firmly intend, with your help,
to do penance, to sin no more,
and to avoid whatever leads me to sin.
Our savior Jesus Christ suffered and died for us.
In his name, my God, have mercy.

The Angelus

The angel of the Lord declared unto Mary,
And she conceived of the Holy Spirit.
    Hail Mary . . .
Behold the handmaid of the Lord,
Be it done unto me according to your word.
    Hail Mary . . .
And the Word was made flesh,
And dwelt among us.
    Hail Mary . . .
Pray for us, O Holy Mother of God, that we may be
    made worthy of the promises of Christ.
Let us pray: Pour forth, we beseech you, O Lord,
    your grace into our hearts that we to whom the
    incarnation of Christ, your Son, was made
    known by the message of the angel may, by
    his passion and cross, be brought to the glory
    of his resurrection, through Christ our Lord. Amen.

Memorare

> Remember, O most gracious Virgin Mary, that it never was known that anyone who fled to your protection, implored your help, or sought your intercession was left unaided.
> Inspired by this confidence, I fly to you, O Virgin of Virgins, My Mother.
> To you I come, before you I stand, sinful and sorrowful.
> O Mother of the Word Incarnate, despise not my petitions, but in your mercy, hear and answer me. Amen.

Because of Mary's singular cooperation with the action of the Holy Spirit, the Church loves to pray in communion with the Virgin Mary, to magnify with her the great things the Lord has done for her, and to entrust supplications and praises to her.

CCC 2682

$\mathscr{R}$ECOMMENDED $\mathscr{R}$ESOURCES

$\mathscr{M}$OST AUTHORS WHO INCLUDE a list of recommended resources generally do so without revealing the criteria they've used. I'm happy to reveal mine. Here I've included references I found useful while researching and writing this book. Please be forewarned that these resources differ widely in quality. Still, many offer decent content; a few are quite wonderful to read through, but I'll let you be the judge. I'd also like you—and my mother— to know that the allegedly doctrinal perspectives of some cited websites give me the willies, but I've included them anyway.

Books

Ball, Ann. *A Handbook of Catholic Sacramentals*. Huntington, Indiana: Our Sunday Visitor Publishing Division, 1991.

Bradner, John. *Symbols of Church Seasons and Days*. Harrisburg, Pennsylvania: Morehouse Publishing, 1977.

Bur, Jacques. *How to Understand the Virgin Mary*. New York: Continuum, 1996.

Catechism of the Catholic Church (Second Edition). Liberia Editrice Vaticana, 1997.

Davidson, Gustay. *A Dictionary of Angels*. New York: The Free Press, 1967.

Dues, Greg. *Catholic Customs and Traditions*. Mystic, Connecticut: Twenty-Third Publications, 2001.

Forest, Jim. *Praying with Icons*. Maryknoll, New York: Orbis Books, 1997.

Gould, Meredith. *Come to the Table: A Catholic Passover Seder for Holy Week*. Plowshares Publishing, 2004.

Gould, Meredith. *Deliberate Acts of Kindness: Service as a Spiritual Practice*. New York: Doubleday/Image, 2002.

Greeley, Andrew. *The Catholic Imagination*. Berkeley and Los Angeles: University of California Press, 2000.

Groeschel, Fr. Benedict J. *The Rosary: Opening Our Hearts to the Mysteries of Faith*. St. Louis, Missouri: Creative Communications for the Parish, 1995. (Booklet)

Hynes, Mary Ellen. *Companion to the Calendar*. Chicago, Illinois: Liturgical Training Publications, 1993.

Isca, Kay Lynn. *Catholic Etiquette: What You Need to Know about Catholic Rites and Wrongs*. Huntington, Indiana: Our Sunday Visitor Publishing, 1997.

Johnson, Kevin Orlin. *Rosary: Mysteries, Meditations, and the Telling of the Beads*. Dallas: Pangaeus Press, 1996.

Johnson, Kevin Orlin. *Why Do Catholics Do That?* New York: Ballantine Books, 1994.

National Conference of Catholic Bishops. *Catholic Household Blessings & Prayers*. Washington, D.C.: NCCB/USCC, 1989.

Panati, Charles. *Sacred Origins of Profound Things.* New York: Arkana/Penguin, 1996.

Pilarczyk, Daniel E. *Practicing Catholic.* Cincinnati: St. Anthony Messenger Press, 1999.

Redemptorist Pastoral Publication. *The Essential Catholic Handbook: A Summary of Beliefs, Practices, and Prayers.* Liguori, Missouri: Liguori, 1997.

Rest, Friedrich. *Our Christian Symbols.* Cleveland: The Pilgrim Press, 1982.

Rohr, Richard, and Joseph Martos. *Why Be Catholic? Understanding Our Experience and Tradition.* Cincinnati: St. Anthony Messenger Press, 1989.

Stravinskas, Rev. Peter M.J. (editor). *Our Sunday Visitor's Catholic Encyclopedia.* Huntington, Indiana: Our Sunday Visitor Publishing Division, 1991.

Walsh, Mary Caswell. *The Art of Tradition: A Christian Guide to Building a Family.* Denver: Living the Good News, Inc., 1998.

Weber, Christin Lore. *Circle of Mysteries: The Women's Rosary Book.* St. Paul, Minnesota: Yes International Publishers, 1995.

Weigel, George. *Letters to a Young Catholic.* New York: Basic Books, 2004.

Internet Resources

Here's an extremely brief refresher course about how to find stuff on the Internet. First, log on to a search engine. I rely almost totally on Google (www.google.com) for a variety of reasons, not the least of which includes using "google" as a verb. I digress.

Once you're linked to a search engine, slug in one or more key words and then see what pops up. Use broad, general terms (e.g., "Catholic calendar") if you have time to wander through a huge treasure trove. Otherwise, be specific with names, titles, categories, or activities (e.g., "making Jesse Tree ornaments"). Here are some sites to get you started:

General Catholic Sites

Find news and information about all things Catholic from a variety of perspectives, some of which purport to be "official":

www.catholic.com (Catholic Answers)
www.catholic.net
www.catholicity.com
www.catholicevangelism.org
www.catholicexchange.com
www.catholicnews.com
www.catholic.org (Catholic Online)
www.catholic-pages.com
www.cin.org (Catholic Information Network)
www.cwnews.com (Catholic World News)
www.ewtn.com
www.godspy.com
www.ncronline.org (National Catholic Reporter)
www.newadvent.org
www.silk.net/RelEd
www.usccb.org (United States Conference of Catholic Bishops)

Catechism of the Catholic Church

Even though I think it's actually easier to thumb through 904 pages of the published text, here's the authorized online site for the English version:

www.scborromeo.org
www.vatican.va

The Catholic Calendar

Generate the liturgical calendar, find dates for moveable feasts, and find out more about the ecclesiastical year you'll want to observe, now that you've read my book.

www.easterbrooks.com/personal/calendar
www.romcal.net

The Daily Office, Prayers, and Devotionals

Pray the Liturgy of the Hours according to the proper lectionary cycle, the Rosary, and discover other Catholic prayers:

www.amm.org (Association of the Miraculous Medal)
www.catholic-forum.com (The Catholic Community
    Forum)
www.catholic-pages.com
www.monksofadoration.org
www.prayrosary.com
www.therealpresence.org
www.trialofamerica.com
www.universalis.com

www.usccb.org/publishing/liturgy/mary.html
www.webdesk.com/catholic/prayers/

Catholic History, Traditions, and Customs

Learn more than you can imagine ever knowing about Catholic heritage and practice. Discover new things to care about:

www.americancatholic.org
www.catholicmom.com
www.catholicmoms.com
www.crossroadsinitiative.com
www.domestic-church.com
www.holyspiritinteractive.com
www.holytrinitygerman.org
www.theholidayspot.com
www.udayton.edu/mary (The Mary Page)
www.whychristmas.com
www.wf-f.org (Women for Faith and Family)

Liturgical Arts

Learn how to praise God through arts and crafts:

www.swiftsite.com/angelwings/cantor.htm (Keep up with your cantor!)
www.iconofile.com
www.nb.net/~pearson/
www.prosoponschool.org
www.rosarymart.com

www.rosaryparts.com
www.surmastore.com

Stuff

Enrich your home with images, flavors, music, and scents:

www.apirecords.com
www.catholiccompany.com
www.catholicfamilycatalog.com
www.catholicstore.com
www.catholicgreetings.org
www.catholicpages.come
www.catholicshopper.com
www.christmas-cookies.com
www.comeandseeicons.com
www.cornerstonecatholic.com
www.getfed.com
www.iconsandmore.com
www.inhisname.com
www.justcatholic.com
www.leafletonline.com
www.monasteryicons.com
www.oplatki.com
www.paxhouse.com
www.religiousmall.com
www.stgabriel.com

INDEX

© Paul Schindel

ABOUT THE AUTHOR

Meredith Gould, Ph.D., is the author of five books, including *Come to the Table: A Catholic Passover Seder* and *Deliberate Acts of Kindness: Service as a Spiritual Practice*. A convert to Catholicism, she brings a fresh appreciation of age-old customs and provides a framework for understanding the symbols and celebrations of her chosen faith. Dr. Gould lives in Princeton, New Jersey, and welcomes reader comments on her website, www.meredithgould.com.

Printed in the United States
by Baker & Taylor Publisher Services